THE BIBLE STORY
AND ITS BACKGROUND

Book Six
The Parables of Jesus

THE BIBLE STORY

AND ITS BACKGROUND Book Six

The Parables
of Jesus

NORMAN J. BULL, Ph.D.

Illustrated by Grace Golden, A.R.C.A.

HULTON EDUCATIONAL PUBLICATIONS

Titles in this series

OLD TESTAMENT TITLES

NEW TESTAMENT TITLES

© NORMAN BULL 1969

71750452 2

First published 1969 by Hulton Educational Publications Ltd.

55/59 Saffron Hill, London, E.C. 1

Printed in the German Democratic Republic

Contents

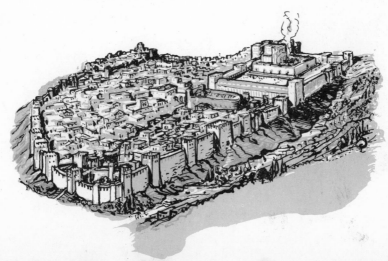

Jesus the Teacher

Stories

Jesus was a born story-teller. Stories like THE GOOD SAMARITAN and THE PRODIGAL SON are among the most popular in the whole world. Everyone, young or old, loves a story. But Jesus did not tell stories just because people like them. Every story he told was a teaching story. Every one teaches something about God, or about men, or about God and men.

Why did Jesus teach through stories? For one thing, he was a Jew and the Jews always taught in stories. There are some in the Old Testament—the "Bible" of the Jews. There are many in the teachings of the Jewish Rabbis—the scholars who taught the Law of God. Jews thought in pictures. They imagined everything in picture form. When they wanted to describe God, for example, they said—God is like a father, or a king, or a judge, or a potter, or a shepherd, or a carpenter. Men were likened to God's children, or his servants, or his debtors. The Jews, the people of God, were likened to a vineyard, or a fig-tree, or a flock of sheep. Jesus thought in this way, too. We shall find many of these likenesses in the stories he told.

All the stories of Jesus were naturally about the world in which he lived. That is why they give us such a wonderful picture of life in Palestine in his day. Because Jesus was a countryman, most of his

7

stories are about life in the countryside—on the land, in the fields, in the village, in the market town. He was talking to people about things they knew well. No wonder they loved to listen to his teaching so much.

But people had to do more than just listen to the stories of Jesus and enjoy them. They had to think about each story. By thinking about it they saw how it applied to them. Very often Jesus put a story in question form, or ended it with a question. The listener had to think before he could answer. His answer brought out the truth in the story. Jesus knew that some people would hear his stories but would not see the truth which they taught. But there was no better way of teaching and of making people think.

There was another reason why Jesus told stories about daily life. To him everything spoke of God, for everything had been created by God. The Jews were like some people today who look for God only in wonders and miracles. Jesus taught them to see God at work in the everyday things of life—the birds, the wild flowers, the rising sun, the falling rain, the growing seed. "Look," Jesus said to the anxious, worried people sitting and listening to him. "Look at Brother Raven in the sky above you. He does not plough or sow or reap. He has no barns to store his harvest. God gives him all he needs. If he cares so much for the birds of the air, how much more will he care for you! Or look at Sister Anemone, growing here wild at your feet, covering the hillside with a carpet of beauty. These wild flowers do not toil at spinning and weaving. Yet even great King Solomon, in his royal purple, was never dressed so magnificently. God gives these flowers their beauty. Will he not much more give you, his children, what you need? Don't worry. Don't be anxious. Trust him—he will provide for you!"

8

Jesus saw God at work in nature. He saw God at work in human nature, too. Jesus did not have to think up stories to describe God and his kingdom. He saw them all around him.

The stories of Jesus were taken from life. They were true to life in his day. But, because human nature is always the same, they are true to life in our day. We can see ourselves in them. They apply to us just as much as they did to the Jews in Palestine long ago. We can learn from them, too.

Parables

These stories of Jesus are called PARABLES. This word comes from the Greek word PARABOLE. It means comparing two things—putting them side by side. A PARABLE is a COMPARISON. That is why many of the parables of Jesus begin "The kingdom of God is like. . ."

The simplest kind of parable is a short saying—"You are the light of the world." These picture sayings are just like our proverbs. Jesus was comparing his disciples to a light. When we say "a rolling stone gathers no moss", we are comparing a shiftless man to a stone. A teacher might say to a stubborn boy, "What a donkey you are." In all these sayings there is a comparison—setting two things side by side. They are picture sayings.

In the second kind of parable more detail is added. Here there is a clear comparison. After Jesus had said, "You are the light of the world", he went on, "Men do not light the family lamp and then put it under the bed or under the measuring tub. Of course not. They put it on the lamp-stand so that everyone in the house can see. Let your light shine like that. Men will see the goodness of God shining in you and they will give glory to him."

Scribe

PEOPLE IN THE
TIME OF JESUS

High Priest

Pharisee

Priest

A Roman
Soldier

A Roman
Centurion

A Roman Governor

A Roman Governor's
Wife

A Villager

A Villager's Wife

A Beggar

A Rich Townsman

A Well-to-do Farmer

A Shepherd

A Fisherman

A Potter

A Farm-worker scattering seed

A Ploughman

CHILDREN IN THE TIME OF JESUS

Riding the family donkey

A shepherd boy with his sling

Playing at Processions

Going with mother to the well

At meal time

The third kind of parable is a complete story. It may be short or long. There is more detail in it—much more than in the picture saying or the simple comparison. Most of the famous parables are stories of this kind.

Allegories

If we are to understand the parables of Jesus we must remember one thing. Each parable teaches only one truth. The details do not matter. We must look for the one truth and not bother about the details.

There is another kind of story called ALLEGORY. In an allegory every character and every detail stand for something else. The most famous allegory is *Pilgrim's Progress* written by John Bunyan. He tells how the travellers came to the House Beautiful. The ladies who lived there were Prudence, Piety and Charity. The maid is Discretion. The bed-chamber is Peace. Everything stands for something else.

Paul told an allegory about a Roman soldier. Every piece of his equipment stood for something else. His belt is truth, his breast-plate is righteousness, his shield is faith, his helmet is salvation, his sword is the spirit of God.

An allegory is just the opposite of a parable. Some people have tried to turn the parables of Jesus into allegories. This is quite wrong. We must look for the one truth the parable teaches. We must ignore the details and not try to make each detail stand for something else. We shall see how important this is.

The kingdom of God

Because there are different kinds of parables scholars do not agree

13

as to how many there are in the Gospels. Some say there are only 27. Others say there are as many as 59. The number generally agreed is 39.

Some of the simple sayings may have been common among the Jews in the time of Jesus. Some of his parables may have been taken from real life, and others made up. None of this matters a bit. What does matter is the truth Jesus was teaching in the parable he told.

In his parables Jesus was teaching about the kingdom of God—or, as it called in Matthew's Gospel, the kingdom of heaven. By this Jesus meant the rule of God in the hearts of men. If a man loves God and obeys him, then God rules in his heart. God is his king and he is God's subject. All those who accept God as king are members of his kingdom. Jesus taught us to pray that God's kingdom may come on earth as it is in heaven—that God may rule in the hearts of all mankind.

Jesus did not invent the idea of the kingdom of God. When he lived in Palestine the Jews looked forward eagerly to the coming of God's kingdom on earth. Their prophets of old had given them a great hope of a deliverer or saviour whom God would send to his people. The Hebrew word for this saviour was MESSIAH—the ANOINTED ONE or KING. In Greek this became CHRISTOS and in English CHRIST. When the Messiah came he would set up God's kingdom on earth. It would be a kingdom of peace and of righteousness and of love.

By the time of Jesus the Jews hoped for quite a different kind of Messiah. They had suffered terribly as a nation. They wanted an earthly kingdom of power and glory. Many thought that the Messiah would be a mighty warrior, like King David of old, who would drive out the Romans and set up a great Jewish kingdom. Many thought that the Messiah would come on the clouds of heaven, with great signs and wonders. Everyone looked forward to his coming.

Jesus was the Messiah of God, the saviour foretold by the prophets. He was not the kind of Messiah the Jews longed for. With him the kingdom of God had come on earth and he called men to enter into it. He knew that the kingdom could not be established by war or by wonders—only by love. The Jews could not understand this kind of Messiah. The religious leaders saw Jesus only as a trouble-maker. He threatened everything they stood for. He threatened their peace with the Romans, too. They had to get rid of him. But Jesus left the seed of the kingdom in the hearts of his disciples. That seed has gone on growing ever since.

Jesus did not only tell stories about the kingdom of God. He showed it in his life—in his perfect love and in his perfect obedience to the Father.

Understanding the parables

Jesus spoke in the Aramaic language. When his parables came to be written down they were written in Greek—the common language of the world at that time. Small details were changed in the Greek version—especially by a man like Doctor Luke who was himself a Greek. This is one reason why scholars have had to work hard to find out the actual stories Jesus told.

Aramaic writing

Greek writing

There are other reasons, too. Many of the parables were told to the enemies of Jesus—proud Pharisees, worldly priests, and wily scribes. But the Church used them to teach the followers of Jesus. Christians sometimes interpreted the parables in a different way. They added new endings or conclusions, and gave them different meanings. They began to turn the parables into allegories. We can even see this in the Gospels themselves, and they were written within about 50 years of the earthly life of Jesus.

Jesus spoke with great urgency. He had brought the kingdom of God into the world. The Jews had to decide quickly whether they would accept him as the Messiah, or not. That is why many of his parables are about the crisis he had brought into the world. But, as the Christian Church grew and spread, these parables were used in a new way. They were used to teach Christians how to live in the kingdom of God. Now they were not stories of crisis and decision. They were stories to teach Christians to be humble and forgiving, to love God and to love their fellow men.

Now you can see why the parables of Jesus are not such simple stories as some people imagine. To understand them we have to come as near as we can to the actual words of Jesus. Above all, we have to know about life in Palestine in the time of Jesus. That is why this book is all about the daily life of the Jews.

Sometimes Jesus did not tell parables—he acted them. He rode into Jerusalem on a donkey; he turned the traders out of the temple; he washed his disciples' feet; he set a child before them. These were acted parables—perhaps you can think of others, too. But in this book we shall be finding out about the parables which Jesus told, and about the kingdom of God which they made known to men.

To look up

Find and read these two parables in the Old Testament:

The ewe lamb   2 Samuel 12.1-14.

The vineyard   Isaiah 5.1-7.

See if you can explain what these parables meant.

To find out

Here are some references. Find out from them different ways in which the Jews thought of God.

Isaiah 40.11; Ezekiel 34.11-15.

Jeremiah 31.32.

Psalm 103.13; Malachi 2.10; Hosea 11.1.

Jeremiah 18.5-6.

Which of these do you think is the best picture of God? Find out more about it. Say why you think it describes God best.

To read

If you have not yet done so, read John Bunyan's allegory called *Pilgrim's Progress*.

John Bunyan

Christian with Prudence, Piety and Charity giving him his armour

Find Paul's allegory of the Roman soldier in Ephesians 6.13-17. Draw a Roman soldier and write in what each part of his equipment represents.

To find in your dictionary

Look up in your dictionary the words METAPHOR and SIMILE. These are very similar to parables and will help you to understand them better. Make sure you write down the meanings of all these three words in your word-list.

To look up

Look up these references to the word Christ or Messiah:
John 1.40-41; John 4.25-26.
Mark 8.27-30; Matthew 16.16-17.
Add these words and their meaning to your word-list.

To collect

Make your own collection of proverbs or picture sayings and see how many you can find.

The Jews loved proverbs and there is a book of them in the Old Testament. Some of our proverbs come from it. You can add these to your collection—Proverbs 2.6; 3.5-6; 12.22; 13.24; 15.1; 15.13; 16.8; 16.16; 16.18; 17.17; 17.22; 20.13; 22.6.

Proverbs 13.24

INTERIOR OF A PEASANT HOME

Home Life

Homes

Jesus himself had grown up in a simple cottage home in Galilee. He knew all about the life of the peasants. Many of his parables were about homes and home life.

Home life was very important to the Jews. It was many centuries since they had been nomads and wanderers. They were not fond of travelling and they hated the sea. Home was the centre of their life. They loved large families, for a man's good name lived on in his children. They were a blessing from God, the best kind of wealth a man could have. Not to marry was almost a crime. To have no children when you did marry was a dreadful disgrace. The rabbis said that a man without children was as good as dead.

Children were brought up strictly but it was for their own sakes. They were greatly loved but not spoilt. In their homes they learnt to know and to love the God of their people and to walk in his ways.

Houses

In the time of Jesus there were fine houses in Palestine. At Jericho have been found the ruins of a palace built by Herod the Great. It had courts with colonnades, rooms at different levels, terraced gardens with fountains, a theatre and a swimming-pool. Herod also built a fortress-palace at Masada. Rich men built their houses

21

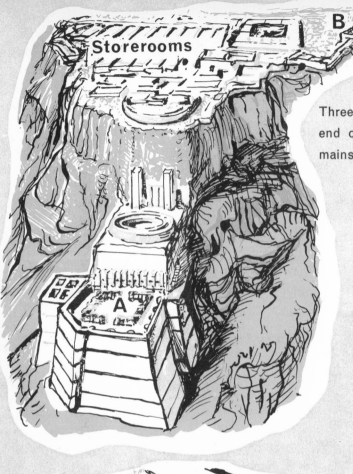

Storerooms

B

HEROD THE GREAT'S

Three terraces at the north end of the rock, with the remains of the palace.

A

650 y

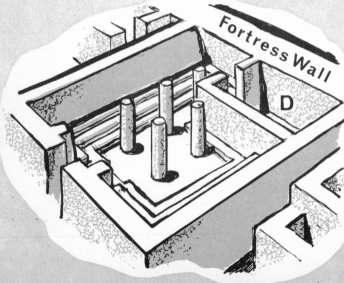

Fortress Wall

D

Reconstruction of a synagogue (B) probably originally built by Herod and later rebuilt by the Zealots in A.D. 66. Scrolls of parts of Ezekiel and Deuteronomy (one being exactly the same as a scroll found at Qumram) were found under the floor.

PALACE AT MASADA

The rock of Masada, with the zigzag path used by Herod to enter the Palace.

A reconstruction of part of the Pavilion or Banqueting Hall (A), reached by staircases cut in the rock. Frescoes are painted to imitate marble.

A mosaic on the floor of one of the rooms in the Western Palace (C).

round a court, with separate rooms opening on to it. These houses were made of limestone and they were very cool.

But Jesus came from a poor peasant home and the people of Galilee were working folk who lived a hard, simple life. Their houses were very simple. Some were made out of caves, hollowed out of the limestone rock, with the house built on to it. Most were made of wattle and daub, or of baked bricks made of clay and straw and whitewashed with lime.

The peasant house was simply one room divided into two parts. The animals were tethered on the lower part. The family lived and slept on a raised platform.

Roofs

The Jews were very sociable people. Except in winter, they spent most of their spare time out of doors, chatting with their friends and neighbours. They talked in the garden, if they had one. But gardens were very few in a walled city—even rich men like Joseph of Arimathea had gardens outside the walls. Often friends talked in the courtyard, where the cooking was done.

The favourite place for meeting was the flat roof of the house. Here people could enjoy the cool evening breeze after the heat of the day. Jesus spoke of "shouting from the house-tops", broadcasting to the whole village.

A few beams supported the roof which was made of dried mud and brushwood, renewed every year. It would be easy to make a hole in it—as four men did when they wanted to let their sick friend down in front of Jesus in a crowded house. The roof had only a slight slope—just enough to carry the rain into the gutters. The law ordered that every roof must have a parapet all round it so that no one should fall off. If anyone did fall, the owner of the house was guilty. The stairway up to the roof was on the outside of the house.

Some people put up a tent on the roof for sleeping in the hot weather. Rich men built another room on the flat roof. It was used for entertaining—for visitors and parties. It was called the "upper room" or the "guest-chamber". It was in such a room that Jesus and his disciples held the Last Supper.

Foundations

The most important part of any house is its foundations. The Jews realised this and always aimed to build on solid rock. Their cement was a mortar made of clay, shells, and potsherds ground to powder.

Jesus told a parable about two men who each built a house. One was a sensible man. He went on digging down till he came to hard rock. Only then did he begin to build his house. The other was a foolish man, too lazy or too stupid to dig down for rock. He built his house on sand. When the two houses were finished they looked much the same.

Then came the rains. In Palestine the rains fell twice a year— the Former and the Latter rains of October and March. Average rain-fall is 16 inches a year, over 20 inches in Galilee. But it all falls in a very few days in violent storms. Soon the rain was teeming down into the valley where these two houses stood. The dried-up

The stone, outside stairway led
up to the flat roof which was
very popular. It had many uses.
Children played there. People
talked there, in the cool of the
evening, and sometimes slept
there. It was a place for quiet
thought or prayer. It was used
for drying fruit such as dates
and figs. Housewives used it
for drying and grinding grain,
for baking and cooking, for
spinning and weaving.

PEASANT HOUSE

We have a saying, 'Don't shout it from the housetops.' This comes from the Bible. Merchants shouted their wares from the roofs of houses near the market (Luke 12.3).

The roof of a peasant house was made simply of brushwood and mud, laid over wooden beams, and rolled smooth. It was cracked by the heat of summer and had to be repaired before the winter rains. It was quite easy to make a hole in the roof (Mark 2.1-12).

wadi, or river-bed, became a raging torrent swirling round the houses while the gale hurled itself at them. The house built on rock had solid foundations and it weathered the storms. But the sand beneath the other house was sucked away and it fell with a resounding crash.

This parable came at the end of the teaching of Jesus which we call the Sermon on the Mount. It was a simple comparison. Men are like those builders. Those who build their lives on the teaching of Jesus have strong foundations. They will stand firm in the storms of life. But others hear his teaching and ignore it. They build their lives on sand. They have no foundations to their lives and, when the storms of life come, they suffer disaster.

Light

The peasant house was a simple cube in shape. It was built to keep out the sun, and therefore it had little light coming into it. It was, in fact, quite dark.

There was only one door and it was narrow. Jesus said that the door to eternal life with God is narrow, and that not many find it. The door was low, too. "Making your door higher" was a Jewish saying for "showing off."

Nor was there much light to be got from windows. Rich men's houses did have a kind of glass, but no peasant could afford that. His house had only one window, if that. It was quite high up in the wall which faced the street. It was a very small window, for a large opening would let in sun and wind and rain. It would let in thieves, too.

The peasant house was so dark that the lamp was kept burning most of the time. The lamp was useful for lighting a fire, for cooking in the courtyard, or for kindling a charcoal fire in a brazier when it was very cold. It was kept alight all night, too, for the Jews did not like the dark.

Jesus only ever refers to "a lamp" or "the lamp." He knew that humble folk could not afford more than one. It was made of clay and it was round or oval in shape, with a handle for carrying. It had two holes on the top—one for the wick, made of flax, and the other for pouring in the olive oil. Cleaning and filling the lamp was an important job every day. Jesus probably did it when he was a boy. The lamp was placed either in a hole made for it in the wall or on a stand made of pottery or metal.

Jesus said to his disciples, "You are the light of the world." Two short parables showed what he meant by this comparison. One was: "A city set on a hill cannot be hid." Jesus may have been thinking of Jerusalem, which was built on a rocky plateau 2,500 feet high. It is the highest capital city in the world. A Jewish poet described Jerusalem as "Beautiful in its height, the joy of the whole earth" (Psalm 48.2). But Jesus said this in Galilee, and he may have been thinking of a small Galilean town called Safed. It was built high on a hill and it could be seen for miles around.

The other parable was about the lamp. "When you light the lamp," Jesus said, "you do not put it under the measuring tub or under the bed, do you? Of course not. You put it on the lamp-stand so that it lights up the whole room. You are to be like the lamp. Let men see the goodness of God shining brightly in you. Then they will give glory to him."

Lamps

Floors

The floors of palaces were made of costly cedarwood or cypress. Rich men's floors were made of pebbles, or of clay tiles baked in the oven. But in the houses of peasants the floor was simply the rock on which the house was built, or just beaten earth with no covering.

Jesus told a parable of a peasant woman who lived in such a house. She had lost a coin. It was a Greek drachma, worth about 2/6d or 12½p in English money. It had fallen from the circlet which she wore round her forehead. This had been a wedding gift and it was a family treasure, so that it was doubly precious. The coin must have fallen off in one of the dark corners of the room. The woman lit the lamp. Then she took out her broom, made of palm leaves, and began to sweep the dusty floor. As she swept she listened carefully for the tinkle of the coin. At last she found it and eagerly scooped it up. She was so excited and happy that she rushed out to call her friends and neighbours. They were just as happy as she was when they heard the good news. What rejoicing there was!

Heaven is just like that, Jesus said. The angels of God are just as happy and joyful when a man who has been lost to God turns back to him again. The coin was a small one but it was precious to that woman. The man might seem a nobody but he is precious to God.

Jesus told this parable to the Pharisees. They were very pious men but some were proud and haughty. They were so sure of their own goodness that they despised those who were not so religious. They were disgusted at the way Jesus went after outcasts and sinners and hobnobbed with them. But Jesus was doing God's work. There is more joy in heaven over one sinner who repents than over ninety-nine pious men who think they are pleasing to God.

Ornaments were worn among the Jews by both men and women. Jewellery was very popular, as well as valuable, for it was a safe way of keeping wealth. Women often wore a kind of head-band made of coins. It was a wedding present so that it was doubly valuable. It was also the family bank. For a woman to lose one of these coins, as in the parable of Jesus, was a dreadful loss.

Bread

One of the main tasks of the housewife was to prepare daily meals for her family. Bread was the most important part of any meal. In the Hebrew language "to eat bread" meant "to have a meal".

The rich man's bread was made from wheat, the poor man's bread was made from barley. Women ground the grain between two millstones in the courtyard, and then kneaded the dough in a trough. To make the dough rise they used fermented dough left over from the last baking. Only a little yeast was needed for three pecks of flour—the usual amount used in baking for the family. But it leavened all the dough. That was why Jesus said that the kingdom of God is like leaven. Only a little leaven is enough to influence all the dough and to work right through it. Only a few Christians influence many and spread the faith through all the world. That is how the kingdom of God grows.

Sometimes in the Bible "leaven" stands for bad influence. For example, Jesus told people to "beware of the leaven of the Pharisees". Mostly he used "leaven" to mean good influence. God's kingdom grows on earth through the good influence of those whose hearts are given to him.

Bread was baked in the household oven, made of clay, which was placed on the embers of the fire. Loaves were round, and the bread was broken with the fingers, not cut with a knife. Today, as in Bible times, three small loaves make a meal for one. In a hot climate bread quickly turns mouldy. That was why the housewife baked bread for her family early every morning.

Sleeping

It happened, said Jesus, in another parable, that a man arrived at his friend's house late one night. He had wisely travelled by moonlight so as to avoid the fierce heat of the sun during the day. Now it was late and he needed food and rest for the night. He knew he could rely on his friend. In the East the law of hospitality was sacred. Often a man's life depended on it. No one would ever refuse food and shelter to a stranger, let alone a friend. Gladly the householder welcomed his friend, and took him in. But imagine his horror when his wife told him there was not a loaf of bread in the house! There were no shops in a village in those days. There was only one thing to do. He must borrow some bread from his neighbour. He and his family would be in bed, asleep, at this late hour, of course.

Jewish rabbis said that sleep is a gift from God. It was a sin to lie awake! Rich men slept in the Roman fashion—in fine beds, made of carved wooden frames, and piled with cushions and blankets. Poor men, like this householder, slept on the floor on mats or palliasses filled with straw. These "beds" were rolled up in the morning and stored away in an alcove during the day time. For a pillow they used a piece of wood—or simply a stone neck-rest. Once a man came to Jesus and said eagerly that he would follow Jesus anywhere. Jesus wanted him to count the cost of being a disciple. "Foxes have holes and the birds have nests," Jesus said. "But I have not even a stone to rest my head upon."

Some of these peasant beds were big enough for two or three people to sleep on. It was like that in the neighbour's house. His family were all fast asleep. He would have to wake them up to get the three loaves. His door had been bolted long ago. A bar of wood

A Roman-type bed

BEDS

Head-rest

There are many words used in the Bible for resting-places indoors. Some mean beds for sleeping, others couches for resting in the day-time, others seats for meals. The ancient Egyptians had beds like ours with bedsteads, and so did the Hebrews in Old Testament times. Some were so high that they needed a stool to climb up on them (2 Kings 1.4). They had head-rests made of wood or alabaster, or sometimes bolsters like ours (1 Samuel 19.15-16).

Stone

A peasant bed

Poor peasants could not afford such beds. It has always been their custom in Palestine to sit on cushions on the ground for meals and to sleep on mats or mattresses. These were rolled up in the morning and stored away in an alcove. Jesus would have slept on a bed like this as a boy. But he also spoke of beds like ours (Mark 4.21).

Sick people were carried to Jesus on a pallet. But the paralysed man whom Jesus healed was carried on a simple mat. That was why he could roll it up and carry it home under his arm (Mark 2.12).

In the time of Jesus many Jews followed the Graeco-Roman custom of reclining at meals on couches.

A Pallet

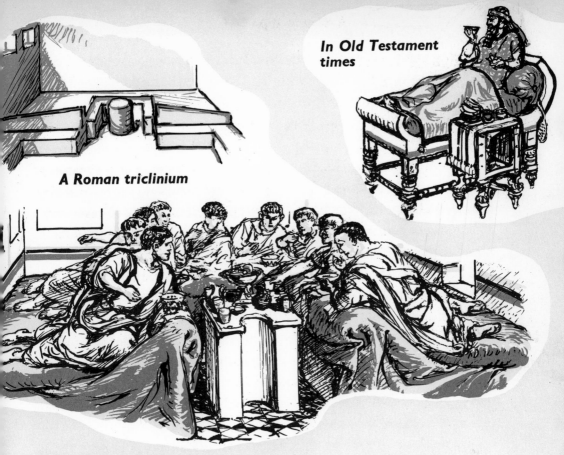

In Old Testament times

A Roman triclinium

The couches were arranged on three sides of the table. In the Roman triclinium, or dining-room, the couches were fixed and held nine diners. The rich Jews arranged their couches in a horseshoe. Guests leaned on the left arm and ate with the right. That was how Jesus was lying when the woman anointed his feet (Luke 7.36-38).

When Jesus and his disciples reclined at the Last Supper so that one of them was 'leaning on Jesus' bosom' (John 13.23-25), he had only to lean back.

6 ft.

Greek-style triclinium followed by the Jews

or iron rested in sockets, or passed through rings, on the two door posts. It was bad enough being woken up in the middle of the night by all that banging on the door and his neighbour crying out for the loan of three loaves. Was he to wake up the whole household as well?

The poor man at the door was quite desperate. The Greek word says that he was "shameless"—he would not go away until he got what he came for. He went on banging and shouting. He knew his neighbour had some bread. By now his family were all awake. He had no excuse left. He would get no peace till he opened the door.

Jesus put this parable in the form of a question. "Just suppose this was what happened", Jesus said. "What would that neighbour do? Would he say—Go away, leave us alone, my family are all in bed? Of course not. It's unthinkable. No one could be so inhospitable. Why, even if he would not get the bread in order to help his friend, he would get it in order to stop all the noise. He would not just give him three loaves. He would give him all that he needs simply because he was so shameless in asking."

Doctor Luke tells us this parable in his gospel. He puts it just after the Lord's Prayer. Jesus had told his disciples how to pray. Now he was telling them to go on asking God for what they needed, like the man who went on knocking and asking for bread. They were to be persistent in prayer. Jesus does not mean that God will give us anything we ask for. Like a good earthly father, God will not spoil us, or make us lazy or greedy. Jesus told us to ask "in his name"—as he would. That is the test of all our prayers.

The neighbour in the parable got out of bed, moved his whole family and hurried to give his friend what he needed. God is just like that—only much more so. He hears our prayers and answers our needs. For he is our Father in heaven who knows and loves and cares for each one of us.

Thieves

Sometimes Jesus spoke about robbers. Everyone knew what he was talking about. He may have been referring to recent happenings. In Palestine then, as in our country today, there were thieves. But in Palestine there were no policemen.

The richer a man was the more he worried about burglars. For, as Jesus said, a man's heart is where his treasure is. "Do not hoard treasure on earth," Jesus said. "Rust bites into fine metal, moths fret at fine clothes, thieves break in and steal. Have your treasure in heaven. Then it will be perfectly safe."

RICH MEN'S HOUSES

Rich men could afford better houses. They were built round an inner court, with separate rooms leading off it. They often had an extra room, built on the flat roof of the house. The outside stairway led up to it. It was very convenient for visitors and it was often known as the 'guest-room' (Mark 14.12-16).

Even poor men's houses were burgled. Windows were few and small, as we have seen, and doors were barred. But it was easy for burglars to burrow a hole in the wall of a peasant house, for it was made simply of clay or of wattle and daub. Thieves came at night when it was dark and everyone was asleep. "If the householder only knew when the thief was coming he would be on guard," Jesus said. "You must always be on your guard, alert and ready for the coming of the Son of Man." Paul said something like this, too, in one of his letters. "The day of the Lord comes as a thief in the night," he wrote.

Jesus often warned his disciples to keep on the alert. He knew that the crisis was coming for himself and his followers. He spoke of the dangers and persecutions they must face. He spoke of the disasters that must come upon Jerusalem. He spoke, too, in a mysterious way of his own return.

The first Christians eagerly awaited this "Second Coming" of Jesus. Still today Christians think of it in the season of the Christian year called ADVENT which means COMING. Still today Christians need to be on guard, ready and alert.

Some robbers were daring enough to attack a rich man's house by day—especially if it were in a lonely spot, deep in the country. Jesus spoke of daylight robbery, too. "If thieves want to rob a strong man's house they must first tie him up," Jesus said. "Then they can plunder his house at leisure." The "strong man" of this parable was the devil. Jews believed in a devil, and in evil spirits or demons dwelling inside a man. They believed that fits and madness were due to being possessed by demons. Jesus, as a Jew, shared these beliefs.

The Pharisees sneered when Jesus cast out demons. "He does it

38

CHART OF THE CHRISTIAN YEAR

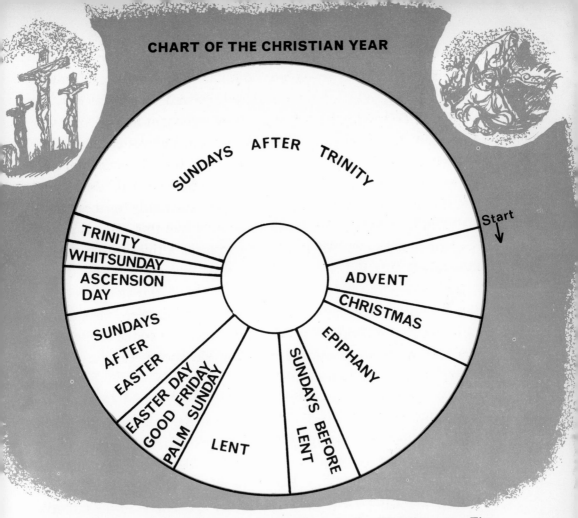

SUNDAYS AFTER TRINITY

Start

TRINITY
WHITSUNDAY
ASCENSION DAY

ADVENT

CHRISTMAS

SUNDAYS AFTER EASTER

EPIPHANY

EASTER DAY
GOOD FRIDAY
PALM SUNDAY

SUNDAYS BEFORE LENT

LENT

This will help you to see where Advent comes in the Christian year. The year begins with the season of Advent about the end of November. This is because the Christian year is based on the life of Jesus, starting with his birthday festival of Christmas. It may seem strange that the Christian year begins at the end of November, when the calendar year begins with January. But there are other 'years' like this—for example, the financial year begins on April 5.

Make your own copy of this chart in your notebook.

through the power of the devil himself," they scoffed. "How can that be?" Jesus replied to them. "If that were so, the devil would be fighting against himself. Only a power stronger than the devil can cast out his demons. Only good can cast out evil. Only the power of God can bind the devil and get back the souls he has seized. But if I cast out devils by the power of God then surely the kingdom of God is here at work among you."

An empty house invited robbers. Jesus told a parable of a landlord who had an evil tenant. He threw him out and had the house done up. It was left clean and polished and tidy—ready for a new tenant. The wicked tenant could not settle anywhere. One day he came back and found his old home empty, ready and waiting. He found seven other ruffians to share his good fortune. They all lived there. The last state of that house was worse than the first.

That parable too was about evil spirits. The house is a man, inhabited by a demon. If it were cast out, his house would be empty. He would need a new tenant, a new master to rule in his heart. If he found none, the wicked tenant would return with seven other devils. To the Jews "seven" was the complete number. Now every kind of wickedness would dwell in that man's heart. His last state would be worse than the first.

This parable was a warning to the Pharisees who were listening to Jesus. "You are hearing the word of God," he said. "Beware you do not ignore it. If you do, you will be like a man set free from one devil who in the end is possessed by many devils. If you do not let my truth dwell in your hearts, you will be far worse off than you were before you heard it."

Salt

The Jews were very fond of seasoning their food. They used many condiments—mustard, mint, coriander, saffron, cummin and rue, for example. Only wealthy men could afford costly pepper, brought all the way from India, or cinnamon, imported from faraway China. Poor people were fond of garlic, onions and shallots. But everyone, rich or poor, needed salt.

Salt came from the Dead Sea—another name for the Dead Sea is the Salt Sea. In Bible times, and still today, salt was obtained in pans by simply letting the water evaporate. It was also mined in the cliffs by the Dead Sea.

Salt was used for seasoning by the Jews because they lived mainly on vegetables. It was also needed to preserve foods such as fish, vegetables and olives. Because it preserves and purifies, it was a symbol of the covenant between God and his people. Perhaps that was another reason why a baby was rubbed with salt at birth. Salt was also a symbol of friendship, for to eat bread and salt with another person was to make a bond between him and you. When an Arab says "there is salt between us", he means "we are friends". Roman soldiers were given a special allowance to buy salt. From the Latin word for this allowance comes our word "salary".

Jesus said to his disciples, "You are the salt of the earth." Just as a little leaven is enough to influence all the dough, and a little salt to preserve all the food, so the little band of disciples were to spread their influence far and wide. "But," Jesus went on, "if the salt decays it is useless. If it loses its taste it is good for nothing. It is thrown away and trodden into the ground." The Jewish people were like that. God had intended them to be the salt of the earth. But they had lost their saltness. The disciples of Jesus were

41

to take their place. They were to be the light of the world, the leaven of mankind, the salt of the earth.

Wine

In a hot country drink is a matter of life and death. Water is precious. As we have seen, Palestine had plenty of rain, but it fell in violent storms in a few days. It rushed through the wadis, or dried-up river beds, and much of it was wasted. Soon the wadis were dry and cracked again once more. The Jews had few reservoirs, and only rich men's houses had piped water. Villagers depended on wells, springs, and streams. Every village had a "master of the waters". When he gave the signal the women hurried to fetch water. They carried it in pitchers or jars on their shoulders. In the towns water-sellers went round the streets carrying water for sale in sewn-up skins.

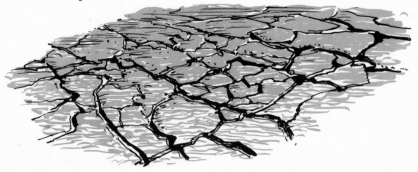

Water from wells and streams was pure and cool, and very refreshing. People also drank milk, vinegar thinned with water, fermented drinks made from fruits, and beer made from barley. But the favourite and most common drink was wine.

Wine is mentioned over 140 times in the Bible. The Jews regarded it as a gift from God, rejoicing a man's heart. It was red wine, and

42

it was always mixed with water. Sometimes two wines were blended together. Often wine was sweetened with honey, and in wealthy homes it was scented after the Greek and Roman fashion.

Wine was kept in tall jars, but more often in wine-skins. These were made from the hides of goats, and the best came from Hebron. The stoppers were made of wood. New wine gives off gases as it ferments. It was safest to put new wine in new skins which were strong and supple. Old wine-skins were stretched and wrinkled. New wine would soon burst them.

"Men do not put new wine into old bottles," Jesus said in another parable. "If they do, the skins burst and both the wine and the skin are lost. New wine is put into new wine-skins." Jesus was referring to his new teaching. Jewish religion was old and worn. Its prophets had looked forward to the coming of the kingdom of God and prepared the way for it. Now the kingdom had come. It was new and powerful. It could not be bottled up in the old religion. The old wine-skins were the Law and the Prophets of Jewish religion. The new wine was the kingdom of God working powerfully among men.

Storing wine in jars

Wine in goatskin bottles

WINE-PRESSES

Jesus in one of his parables described the making of a vineyard (Mark 12.1). It included 'a place for the winefat'. After blossom time in March to April the grapes ripen till the autumn. Then came the happy harvest time in September or later, according to the readiness of the grapes. Some families camped out in the watch-tower during the grape season. Others, men and women and children, came to the vineyard with donkeys laden with baskets (Jeremiah 6.9) to carry the grapes to the wine-press. The bunches were cut with a small pruning-hook (Revelation 14.18). Grape harvest was a very happy time with singing and dancing (Isaiah 16.10).

Some grapes were eaten fresh, some set aside for drying into raisins. Others were boiled to make grape honey, a sweet syrup very precious when sugar was unknown. The winepress was in the vineyard usually. One kind was simply a vat cut in the rock. Some of these have been found and they are quite small, about 6 feet by 9 feet.

Another kind of wine-press was made of limestone above the ground. The workmen trampled the grapes with bare feet (Isaiah 63.2-3), holding on to ropes above their heads, singing and shouting (Jeremiah 25.30). The juice ran into another vat, smaller and deeper. Here it was left for about six weeks so that the stalks and skins and other debris ('the lees') could settle at the bottom.

The wine was drawn off carefully and stored in wine-jars or wine-skins which were then sealed. To put new wine in old wine-skins was asking for trouble.

Clothes

Men wore three garments in the time of Jesus. The main garment was made of linen. It was this that Jesus wore when he washed his disciples' feet at the Last Supper. For he had taken off his outer garment—the cloak or mantle. The tunic was quite long, falling below the knees. Tassels, which were religious symbols, hung from the side seams. A tunic was often made of two pieces of cloth sewn along the hipline. But at Nazareth the weavers had looms large enough to weave woollen tunics in one piece. They were specially valuable. Jesus had one and, when he was crucified, the soldiers diced to see who should have it.

The loose, flowing tunic had to be gathered in with a belt. Belts were made from many different materials according to a man's wealth. They ranged from rope and leather to fine cloth, even silk for the rich. The folds of a cloth belt wound round and round the waist served for pockets.

When a man needed to be energetic, he tucked his tunic up into his belt, leaving his legs free. Workers did this—fishermen, for example. Jesus "girded his loins", as this was called, before he washed his disciples' feet at the Last Supper.

The third garment was a thick cloak, which took the place of our overcoat. It kept out the heat by day and the cold by night. It could serve as a blanket or a bed. It was a rectangular piece of material made of wool or goats' hair or camel hair. A shepherd's cloak was usually striped with brown or black. He could carry a lamb in its folds. If it was held in place by an extra girdle, he could carry corn home from market in this larger "pocket". It was called "in the bosom". "Give, and it shall be given to you," Jesus said. "Good measure, pressed down and running over, shall men give into your bosom."

TALLITHS

Devout Jews had four deep blue tassels hanging from the four corners of their cloaks. These were religious signs of the Jew, marking him off from people of other races. We know that Jesus wore these tassels, for a diseased woman once took hold of the tassels at his back, hoping in that way to receive his healing power. Jesus turned round and asked who had touched his garment (Mark 5.25-34).

The great tallith

The rectangular tasselled cloak was drawn over the head when a Jew prayed, or it could be a separate shawl known as the "great tallith". Today it is worn over a skull cap.

The great tallith, worn for morning prayer only

It was about two yards square. A cord was attached to each corner from which hung eight threads and five knots. They symbolised the commandments of the Law. The prayer shawl was always worn in the synagogue. As the roll of the sacred Law was carried past him, the devout Jew touched it with one of the eight thread tassels of his prayer shawl. Then he kissed the tassel to show his reverence for the sacred scriptures.

The small tallith

Sometimes Jews wore a 'small tallith', a kind of vest, which had the four sacred tassels attached to it. It seems that this was worn in times of persecution. The Jew still wore his sacred symbols, but they were concealed by his outer garments.

A man wearing a "seamless tunic" (seams ending in tassels) and a girdle in which he could carry money and small objects.

One man wearing a cloak and turban, the other in Persian-style coat, hat and shoes.

48

Married women always covered their hair out of
doors. Long veils were worn by Jewish women in
the Assyrian relief of 6th century, see *Prophets of
the Jews*, p. 124 . A cloak could be worn over the
tunic.

An unmarried girl in long tunic and
over tunic. The most valued tunic
was woven in one piece on an upright
loom. Two pieces woven on a hori-
zontal small loom were seamed at
the hips.

Women's sandal found at Masada.
Shoes may have looked like this.

Mantles had tassels at the four corners. A poor man or a nomad, such as Jesus and his disciples were, might have to use his mantle as a prayer shawl.

The costumes worn in Palestine today are the result of the Arab and Turkish conquests after New Testament times, so that we must imagine how they dressed. Some Jews may have adopted Persian-style costume of coat and hat instead of mantle and turban, when they returned from their exile in Babylon.

The Bible uses the same words for the garments of both men and women. Women's clothes were roughly similar to men's. But they were made of finer cloth, they were fuller and longer and better cut, they had sleeves, they were more brightly dyed and they were embroidered. They certainly looked very different from men's, for the Jewish law strictly forbade either sex to wear the clothes of the other. And, of course, women wore such extras as ribbons, shawls, ornaments and jewellery—although men wore jewellery as well. Women wore rings on both fingers and toes, on their ears, and perhaps even in their noses.

No one wore socks. Shoes or sandals were worn on the feet. Shoes were made from the hide of camel or jackal or hyena, and they had soles made from the bark of palm trees or from rushes. Shoes were soft but sandals were made of hard leather and even hobnailed for long journeys. Sandals simply had a sole tied to the foot by a thong or latchet which went over the top of the foot and round the ankle. At home everyone went barefoot. Travellers went barefoot, too, when it was suitable to do so. They saved their sandal leather for the towns.

Linen was made from the flax of Galilee and wool from the sheep of Judaea. Every peasant housewife combed, spun and wove her wool on her own loom to make the family clothes. Those who could afford it paid the weavers and dyers and fullers to do it for them. Wool was cleaned so white that it was a symbol of purity. Jesus came from a poor peasant home where clothes were handed down from father to son and from older children to younger children. He had often watched Mary patching clothes for her large family of at least seven children. This too made a parable. "No one sews new cloth on to an old garment," Jesus said. "If she does, the patch tears away the old cloth and the hole is made bigger." The old garment was the religion of the Jews. The new cloth was the preaching of the kingdom of God which had come into the world with Jesus. It was too strong for the old garment of Jewish religion.

Fathers and sons
We have left till last the most important thing of all—the family itself. The father was the head of the family. The Greek word for father in the New Testament means, "ruler of the house". "Father's house" was another way of saying "the family". In Victorian times in England sons addressed their father as "Sir", and wives addressed their husbands as "Mr". It was like that in a Jewish home. It was a religious duty for a son to obey his father. A wife addressed her husband as "master" or "lord". The father ruled over the house, the family, and all their possessions. Jesus showed that he approved of the sacred commandment of Moses: "Honour thy father and thy mother." He utterly condemned the hypocrisy by which, in the name of religion, a man could get out of supporting his aged parents. Such a man would dedicate all his goods to God, so that he could not use them for any other purpose. Then he could not help his parents.

We have seen how important home-life was to the Jews, and how good it was. Children were brought up strictly, but they were greatly loved. They grew up to honour their parents and to follow their fathers dutifully. But there were exceptions, as two parables of Jesus showed.

The first parable was told by Jesus the day after Palm Sunday. He had ridden into Jerusalem and turned the traders out of the Temple—just as the prophets had foretold. In these two actions he was openly claiming to be the Messiah of God. The religious leaders could not ignore this. So, the next day, when Jesus again appeared

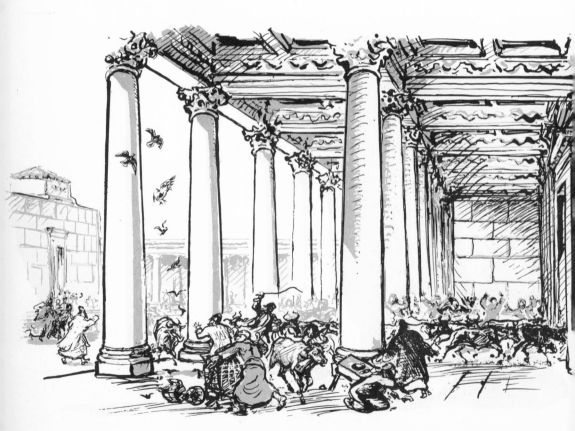

in the Temple, they asked him point-blank, "What is your authority? Who are you claiming to be?" They needed to know urgently. Jesus threatened them and all they stood for, and openly attacked them before the people. Besides, he might well cause trouble with the Romans. He was a double threat to them.

Jesus did not reply directly. He, in turn, asked them a question. "Was John the Baptist sent by God? Or was he just a madman?" This was a terribly difficult question for them to answer. John had called on the Jews to repent and be baptised. Many sinners had turned from their evil ways to follow God's ways. The people had looked up to John as a prophet of God. But the religious leaders had ignored him as a raving lunatic. They dare not answer, in front of the crowd, that they thought John was simply a madman from the desert. But if they said that he had come from God they knew that Jesus would at once say, "Then why did you not believe in him?"

"We cannot answer," they replied to Jesus. "Then I won't answer your question either," Jesus replied. But, though he would not answer them directly, he went on to tell a parable. There was a farmer who had two sons. One morning he went to one son and said, "Son, I want you to go and work in the vineyard today." 'I won't go!', the son replied, rudely. But, some time after, he felt ashamed of his rudeness. He went out and worked hard in the vineyard, as his father had asked. The farmer asked his other son, too. "Of course I'll go, Sir," the son answered, respectfully. But he had no intention of going to work in the vineyard and he never went near it. "Now", asked Jesus, "which of these two was the better son?" "The one who went and worked in the vineyard," the Pharisees replied. "Exactly," Jesus said. "Sinners who turned back to God at the preaching of John are like him. Before that, they had refused to obey God. But when they heard John they were ashamed, they repented, and they began to do the will of God. You are like the other son. You seem to be very respectful to God, dutiful, and obedient to his will. But your religion is insincere, your hearts are far from God, you do not do his will. I tell you that these sinners will go into the kingdom of God before you."

The lost son

The other story which Jesus told of a father and his two sons we call the parable of the "Prodigal Son" or "The Wasteful Son". But this is a bad title. It makes the son seem to be the chief character in the story. He is not. The story's chief character is a loving father, and he is a picture of God, the loving heavenly father. This parable is put with two others in Luke's Gospel—the Lost Coin and the Lost Sheep. We will call it "The Lost Son". For he was lost to his father and it is the father who is important in this parable.

The younger son

A farmer had two sons. One day the younger son came to him and demanded his share of his father's estate. Now according to the law the eldest son inherited a "double portion" of his father's property. Thus, when there were two sons, the elder inherited two - thirds of his father's estate, and the younger son one-third. This was because the elder son was the most important—the family went on through him. Younger sons had to make their own way in the world. Jewish men usually married between the ages of 18 and 20 years. This younger son was unmarried, so that he must have been about 17 years old at the most. He was bored with his father's dull farm. He longed for the excitement of the big, bustling world outside. He demanded the third of his father's property that would come to him sooner or later. Since the house and land must remain in the family they would go to the elder brother. We can imagine that the younger son would be given sheep and goats—for the father, in his love, did not refuse him. He soon sold his inheritance in the market, packed up his money and clothes, and hurried away.

In the time of Jesus most Jews lived outside Palestine. There were four million Jews in other lands. Only half a million at most lived in Palestine. The younger son may have gone to another land, but he did not need to go abroad to find excitement. On the other side of the River Jordan there were the fine Greek cities of the DECAPOLIS—THE LEAGUE OF TEN CITIES. He may have gone to Gerasa or Jerash whose ruins still show what wonderful cities they were. How exciting one of these Greek cities would have been to the young man! They had dazzling shops, a theatre, baths, fine streets and wonderful buildings, a stadium and a hippodrome. These pagan Greeks were full of life and glamour—so different from the narrow-minded Jews, the lad must have thought. Soon he was having a wonderful time. His father's money brought him lots of friends. Life was one round of parties—of music and dancing, feasting and drinking, revelling and making merry.

But his money could not last long at the pace he was living. Soon it was all gone. His fair-weather friends were gone, too. Now he had nothing. He couldn't get a job to keep himself. He was lost in a strange city, alone and friendless, hungry and penniless. He wandered out into the countryside seeking food. A farmer let him look after his pigs as a swine-herd. Greeks and Romans were fond of pigs' flesh. They kept pigs for food and to provide sacrifices for their pagan gods. Jewish Law said that pigs were "unclean"; they must not be used in any way. Jews loathed and despised pigs and would have nothing to do with them. Thus, the younger son was forced by his need to give up his religion. He could not live by the Law or observe the holy Sabbath in his condition. He had to steal food, too. He was so hungry that he would have eaten the carob beans which the pigs lived on, if they had not revolted him so much. No one cared about him. He was a tramp, down and out.

PODS OF THE CAROB TREE

The Bible says that, when all his money was gone, the wasteful son was so hungry that 'he would fain have filled his belly with the husks that the swine did eat'. The Greek word for 'husks' really means 'little horns', and you can see that the pods of the carob tree are shaped like that. They are as much as a foot long. They are sweet and syrupy to eat. They were used in ancient times to fatten cattle. Men ate them too. They are still sold in sweet shops as 'honey beans'. The carob tree needs little moisture; so it spread over the ancient world from Asia Minor. It rises to a height of about 25 feet.

It was then that he came to his senses. He realised, now, what a fool he had been. How much better off he had been at home! There he had been a respected son of the family, wanting nothing, secure in his father's love. He decided to go back home. He realised that his father had no obligation to help him, since he had had his share of the estate. He had no right to ask anything, he knew that. He did not dare to expect his father to receive him back as his son. He would ask him simply to let him come back as a servant.

There were three kinds of servants among the Jews. First there were bond-servants who belonged to the estate. But they were nothing like the slaves of the Greeks and Romans. They were well-treated and the family regarded them with affection. Under them were the ordinary servants. They were at the beck and call of the bond servants, and sometimes were badly treated by them. The third kind were hired servants. They were casual labourers, hired or dismissed at notice. They were the lowest kind of workers, they belonged to no one. The younger son decided to ask his father if he could be one of them.

He hobbled the long miles home in his rags and tatters. His father was the first person to see him, limping in the distance. He recognised him at once. He must often have looked down the road, hoping and longing for his son to return. Perhaps he went up on to the flat roof of the house each day so that he could see further. That may have been why he saw his son first. Despite his age he ran to meet his son—a very strange and undignified thing for an aged and respected Jew to do. He embraced his son lovingly before he could speak. "Father," the son said, when he could get a word out, "I have sinned against you and against God. I am not fit to be called your son. Let me be one of your hired servants."

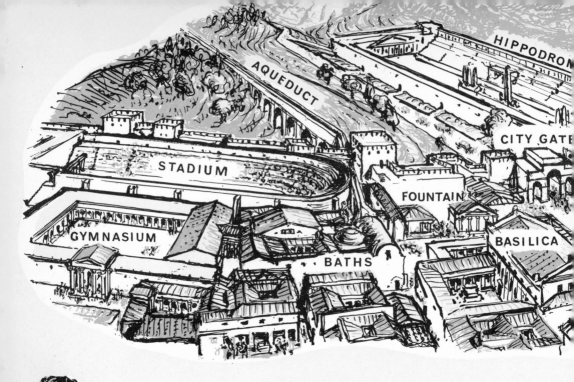

AQUEDUCT

HIPPODROME

STADIUM

CITY GATE

GYMNASIUM

FOUNTAIN

BATHS

BASILICA

GERASA AND THE CITIES OF THE DECAPOLIS

Today at Geresa, now called Jerash, can be seen ruins of fine Roman buildings, which had replaced those of a Greek city of equal magnificence. It was to one of these gay, pagan cities that the younger son would have gone. There were a number of them, east of the river Jordan, joined together in a league called the Decapolis ('Ten Cities').

Temple of Zeus

Roman theatre

Columned street

Roman Forum

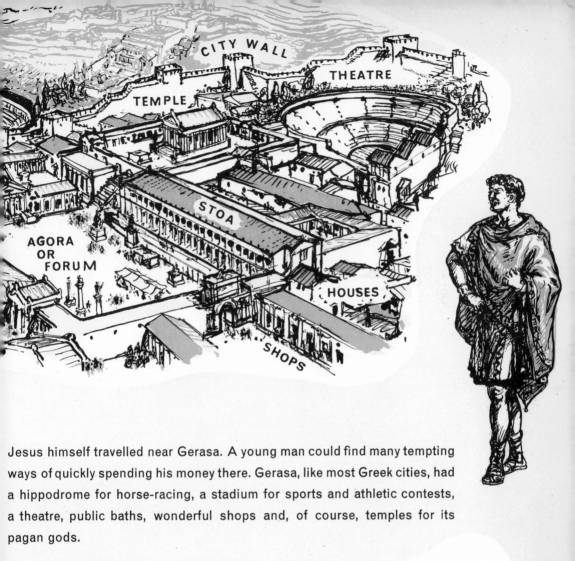

CITY WALL

THEATRE

TEMPLE

STOA

AGORA OR FORUM

HOUSES

SHOPS

Jesus himself travelled near Gerasa. A young man could find many tempting ways of quickly spending his money there. Gerasa, like most Greek cities, had a hippodrome for horse-racing, a stadium for sports and athletic contests, a theatre, public baths, wonderful shops and, of course, temples for its pagan gods.

Hippodrome

His father cut him short. He called out to the bond-servants to bring a fine robe, a ring, and shoes for his dear son. The robe was a costly, ceremonial garment, a symbol of honour. The ring was the father's signet-ring, a sign of authority in the household. Fine slippers, worn only by the family (for servants went barefoot), were a mark of belonging to the family. The wastrel son was being welcomed back as his father's dear son. All was forgiven by the loving father. To him it was as if his son had come back from the dead— it was like finding a lost sheep. He ordered the fatted calf to be killed. That meant a joyous feast for the whole household to celebrate the son's return.

After the feasting came the merry-making. Flutes provided music for the round dance of the men. The noise of the music, the singing, the stamping dance and the loud hand-clapping could be heard a long way off. The elder brother heard it on his way back from a hard day in the fields.

In this parable the father's love was a picture of God's love. The rejoicing in his household was like the rejoicing in heaven when a lost sinner comes back to God. That was why Jesus spent so much time with despised sinners, seeking them out, showing them the love of God. He loved them just as the father loved his foolish son.

The elder son

Religious people like some Pharisees, proud of their goodness, looked down on sinners. They despised Jesus, too, for mixing with them. Jesus added a second part to his parable to answer them. It was about the elder son—a typical Pharisee.

The elder son heard all the din as he came wearily back home that evening. "What's it all about—this music and dancing and

60

Robe

He was an honoured guest.

Ring

He had his father's authority.

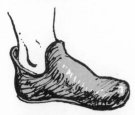

Shoes

He was one of the family; slaves went barefoot

singing?" he called out to a servant. When the servant told him he was furious. He would not go into the house. He certainly wasn't going to share in the rejoicing, just because that lazy, good-for-nothing brother of his had come back. In the end his father had to go out to him and plead with him to come indoors and take his place of honour at the feast. He spoke kindly and lovingly, but his angry son would not even address him courteously. "All these years I've worked for you!" he shouted. "All these years I've obeyed you and served you! You never gave me even a lamb to make merry with my friends! But what happens when this wastrel comes back, after throwing away your money with the riff-raff of the city? Why, you kill the fatted calf and have a grand feast!"

We can easily sympathise with the elder brother because we are human. Our love is limited. But this story is about God and his love has no limits. The elder brother was self-righteous, proud and loveless. "Your son," he said to his father, not "my brother". His heart was hard and bitter. If he had been the father he would have disowned the foolish son completely.

But was the elder brother so right? He had done no more than his duty as a son. The

61

whole estate belonged to him. He was working for himself—all the profits of the farm would come to him. He could have a feast any time he wanted, couldn't he? His father did not mention these facts. He loved his elder son too, and spoke to him with great affection. "My dear son," he said, "I can always rely on you—you are always with me. All that I have is yours. It is your own brother who has come home. It is as if he had come back from the dead. It is like finding a lost sheep. We ought to feast and to make merry to show our great happiness."

The father reproached his elder son for his lack of love in this parable. Jesus, in telling it, was reproaching the Pharisees. They did not love God; they bargained with him. They did not love men; they despised them. But to Jesus nothing else mattered. Love for God and man was the heart of his religion.

Jesus did not only tell parables about God's love. He showed it in the way he lived, for he loved everyone—especially outcasts and sinners. He showed it in the way he died, too. That is why the cross is the symbol of the greatest love the world has ever known.

MUSIC AND DANCING

When the elder brother returned home after his day's work he heard the sounds of music and dancing. There are only three other references to music in the Gospels. There were flute-players at a funeral (Matthew 9.23). Jesus refers to children playing pipes in the market-place (Luke 7.32). He and his disciples sang a hymn (psalm) at the end of the Last Supper (Mark 14.26). But we know that music played a very important part in the life of the Jews. Instruments were used to provide rhythm for dancing and singing, chiefly pipes and drums and tambourines. Music had an important place in worship in the temple and singing in the synagogues. Special times for music and dancing were weddings, funerals and, of course, parties and feasts. Both singing and dancing were done in groups. Sometimes professionals were hired to wail or play flutes at funerals, or to sing and dance at feasts and weddings while the guests looked on.

References for Parables in this chapter

Two builders	Matthew 7.24-27.
The light of the world	Matthew 5.14-16.
The lost coin	Luke 15.8-10.
The leaven in the dough	Matthew 13.33.
The friend at midnight	Luke 11.5-13.
Treasure in heaven	Matthew 6. 19-21.
The thief in the night	Luke 12. 39-40.
The strong man armed	Luke 11. 14-22.
The empty house	Matthew 12. 43-45.
The salt of the earth	Matthew 5.13
New wine in old wine-skins	Mark 2.22.
New patches on old garments	Mark 2.21.
A father and his two sons	Matthew 21. 23-32.
The lost son	Luke 15. 11-32.

Houses

Make a model of a peasant house in Palestine in the time of Jesus. You can use cardboard or wood, covered with alabastine, or wire and paper mâché. Plasticene would be useful for modelling the furniture and animals inside the house.

Two filmstrips called *The Home*, Parts 1 and 2, in the series *Two Thousand Years Ago* (Religious Films Ltd.) show exactly what the peasant home was like.

Find and read in your Bible these references to roofs: Deuteronomy 22.8; Mark 13.15; Matthew 10.27; Luke 22. 11-12. What do they tell us about roofs?

Read in Mark 2. 1-12 how four men broke up the roof of a house to let their sick friend down to Jesus' feet. Why were they able to make a hole in the roof so easily?

The parable of the two builders in Matthew 7.24-27 is really a poem. Write it out, with each phrase on a separate line, and you will see this. Now read this poem together in choral speaking. The best way will be with a swelling chorus. More voices are added as each line is spoken so that the sound swells to a climax ("it fell. . . it fell not").

Make up a story about two children or two people like the two builders. In your story tell how one built his character on a solid foundation and the other had none. Describe what happened to each one.

A HOME MADE OUT OF A CAVE
Still today, as in Bible times, poor folk make their home out of a cave. This house is in Bethlehem.

Light

Read what Jesus said about doors in Matthew 7.13-14. Can you say what he meant by this?

Letter, in illuminated writing if you can, the words of Jesus in Matthew 5.14-16.

Learn by heart Matthew 5.16.

Read how Jesus is described as the "Light of the World" in John 1.9 and John 8.12. There is a famous picture, with this title, by Holman Hunt. See if you can get a postcard copy of it to fix in your notebook. What do you think the artist means by this painting?

Make a model of the kind of lamp used in the time of Jesus. If you make it of clay, and have it baked, you could use a wick of flax and olive oil to light it.

Do not use any other kind of oil.

The good Jewish housewife made sure that her lamp never went out during the night. You can read a description of her in Proverbs 31.10-31.

Write out and learn by heart the saying about the lamp in Psalm 119.105.

What do you think Jesus meant by saying that his followers are to be "the light of the world"? In what ways can we be "lights" to others?

Floors

Mime, or act with your own words, the parable of the lost coin in Luke 15.8-10. In what ways can we be "lost" to God?

Bread

Make a model of the mill-stones used by the peasant women of Palestine.

Read how Jesus broke bread at the Last Supper in Mark 14.22. What did he mean by his saying? Find out about the Service of bread and wine in your own church. Write or tell an account of what happens in this Service.

Each one of us is like leaven—we influence other people. How can

66

we be a good influence to others? After you have talked about this make a list of the ways you have found.

HAND-MILL

Every Jewish housewife had a simple handmill for grinding grain to make bread. It was made of two stones. The lower or nether stone was very heavy and about 18 inches in diameter. The upper millstone went round on a pivot and it was turned by a wooden handle near the edge. The grain was poured into the central hole in the upper stone and ground between the two stones. The meal fell on to a cloth placed under the lower stone.

Grinding was hard work. Women did it in pairs (Matthew 24.41) to make it less tiring. Each gave the wheel a half turn with her left hand and poured grain into the hole with her right hand. Grinding had to be done almost every day for bread did not last long. In wealthy households the slaves did this dreary job.

Sleeping
Act, using your own words, the parable of the friend at midnight in Luke 11.5-13.
Read what Jesus said about God answering our prayers in Luke 11.9-13. Why do you think it seems that sometimes God does not answer our prayers?

Simpler mill or quern found at Masada

Jesus teaches us to be persistent in asking God for what we want. What kind of things do you think we should ask him for? What kind of things should we not ask him for?

Letter, in illuminated writing if you can, the Lord's Prayer from Luke 11.2-4 or Matthew 6.9-13.

Make up a prayer of your own.

Thieves

Read what Jesus said about treasure on earth and in heaven in Matthew 6.19-21. Learn these verses by heart. What kinds of "treasure" should Christians store up in heaven?

Find in your hymnbook the hymns for Advent, about the second coming of Jesus. Read them together in choral speaking. Learn a new one to use in School Assembly when the Advent season comes.

Salt

The saying of Jesus about salt has become one of our proverbs. We say of good people: "they are the salt of the earth". What do you think we mean by this? What kind of people are "the salt of the earth"?

SALT FROM THE DEAD SEA
Still today, as in Bible times, precious salt is obtained from the Dead Sea. Today modern machinery works large evaporating pans.

Wine

Make a model of a wine-jar and a wine-skin to place inside your model house.

Read how Jesus met the need for wine at a wedding-feast in John 2.1-11.

Read what Jesus did with wine at the Last Supper in Mark 14.23-24. What did he mean by his words? If you have not already done so, find out about the service of bread and wine in your own church.

Clothes

Look up these references about clothes—John 13.3-5 and 12-14; John 19.23-24; Mark 1.6; Luke 6.38; Matthew 5.40; Mark 1.7.

Use reference books to find out more about clothes in Palestine and draw or paint people in the time of Jesus to show how they were dressed.

Fathers and sons

Read the parable of the two sons, asked by their father to work in the vineyard, in Matthew 21.23-32.

In what ways do you think we should be obedient to our fathers? After you have talked about this, make up a story to show how children ought to obey their parents. It might be about one sensible child, and one foolish child who was not obedient and fell into trouble.

Act the story of the Lost Son in Luke 15.11-32, using your own words. Or you can draw this parable in a series of pictures as a strip cartoon.

A woman
carrying a jar

A goat-skin,
used for water
and for wine

A man carrying
a skin bottle

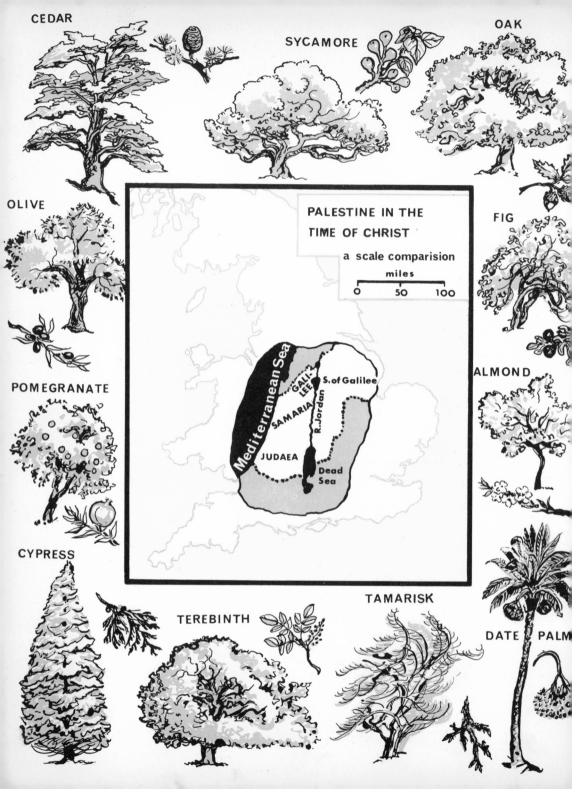

CEDAR

SYCAMORE

OAK

OLIVE

FIG

POMEGRANATE

ALMOND

CYPRESS

TEREBINTH

TAMARISK

DATE PALM

PALESTINE IN THE
TIME OF CHRIST

a scale comparision

miles

0   50   100

Mediterranean Sea

GALI-
LEE

S. of Galilee

SAMARIA

R. Jordan

JUDAEA

Dead
Sea

Country Life

Seed growing secretly

Jesus was a countryman. He had grown up in the countryside of Galilee. He spent much of his ministry in Galilee with people who earned their living from the land. That is why so many of his parables are about country life.

But there was another reason. Jesus saw God at work in nature, just as he saw God at work in men. God had made laws for the life of nature, and laws for the life of men. Those laws were the same. Thus, to Jesus nature was religious. That is why a story from nature was a parable of the kingdom of God.

When the farmer has sown the seed in the earth, Jesus said, he can do nothing more. He just has to be patient and go on with his daily life while he waits for it to grow. It grows mysteriously of its own accord—"automatike" is the Greek word. It grows secretly, according to God's law for its growth. It grows slowly—first the blade, then the ear of corn, and then the grain in the ear. It's no use the farmer worrying; that won't help. Nor is there anything he can do to hasten the harvest—there are no short cuts in nature. He must have faith. He has sown the seed: harvest will come. What a man sows he will surely reap—that is God's law both for nature and for men. Then, when the happy harvest time comes, as it surely will, he takes his sickle and gathers in the grain.

The kingdom of God is just like that, Jesus said. It is like seed

THE WORK OF THE FARMER

1 Sowing

2 Ploughing

3 Irrigating

4 Reaping

5 Transporting

6 Threshing

7 Winnowing

8 Sifting

(Note the order of events – see pages 75-76.)

sown in men's hearts—the kingdom of God is within us. It grows mysteriously, secretly, slowly, according to God's law. God had been sowing the seed among his chosen people through the prophets —the last and greatest of them being John the Baptist. Now it was harvest time and Jesus was gathering it in. "The harvest is plentiful but the labourers are few," he said. He and his little band of disciples were gathering in the people of God into his kingdom.

The mustard seed

Jesus and his disciples were not always welcome, even less so as time went on. The Pharisees had come to hate Jesus for his strange teaching and for his criticisms of them. They were the most religious Jews of all. They lived strictly by the sacred Law. People looked up to them for their piety and for their strict religious lives. They were powerful and they warned the people against Jesus. He became less popular. His disciples were disappointed and began to lose heart. People did not flock to join them in the kingdom of God. The disciples were still few.

Jesus told a parable to help them to understand. It would be just the same with the kingdom of God as it was with a tiny mustard seed—the smallest of all seeds. It was not quite the smallest—the seed of the orchid or of the cypress is tinier. But the mustard seed was so common that the Jews made a proverb from it. Anything very small was said to be "like a grain of mustard seed". If someone tells us a story which we know is false we reply, "There is not a grain of truth in that", meaning a tiny grain of sand or salt or earth. A Jew would say, "There is not a mustard seed of truth in that." Jesus once said, "Even a mustard seed of faith can move mountains." He meant that even a little faith can do great things.

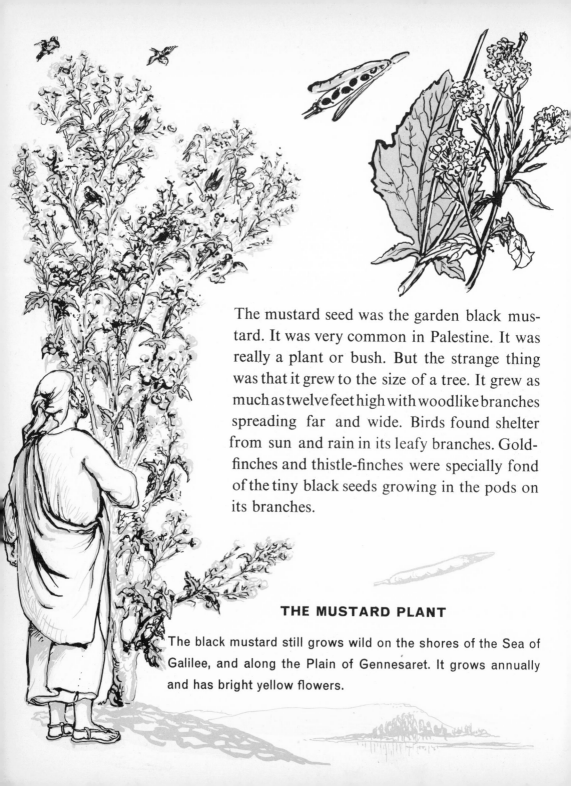

The mustard seed was the garden black mustard. It was very common in Palestine. It was really a plant or bush. But the strange thing was that it grew to the size of a tree. It grew as much as twelve feet high with woodlike branches spreading far and wide. Birds found shelter from sun and rain in its leafy branches. Goldfinches and thistle-finches were specially fond of the tiny black seeds growing in the pods on its branches.

THE MUSTARD PLANT

The black mustard still grows wild on the shores of the Sea of Galilee, and along the Plain of Gennesaret. It grows annually and has bright yellow flowers.

Jesus often spoke of small things and common things. They too had been made by God and they mirrored his ways. They were all parables of the kingdom. People tend to despise small things. That is why the disciples were depressed, for they were few. The parable of the mustard seed answered them. From the tiniest of seeds grew a great tree so that birds from far and near gathered in its branches. From the little band of disciples would grow the great kingdom of God, so that men of all nations would be gathered into it. For, to the Jews, the tree was a symbol of a great kingdom. Just as the tree protected the birds sheltering in its branches, so did an empire protect the states subject to it. The birds were the Gentiles. That is why Jesus said, "They will come from the east and the west, from the north and the south, and sit down in the kingdom of God."

From the twelve patriarchs of the Jews had grown the twelve tribes of the people of God. From the twelve apostles would grow the new Israel—the new people of God. Jesus had brought the kingdom of God on earth. It was open to all—Pharisee and sinner, scribe and tax-collector, Jew and Gentile. All could find shelter under the branches of the kingdom of God.

The Sower

Jesus the countryman knew well that not all the seed which was sown bore a harvest. Everything depended on the soil. He described this in the parable of the sower. It was to help the disciples to understand why so few of the people who heard Jesus took the seed of the kingdom into their hearts and bore harvest.

After the early rains of autumn the farmer sowed his seed. In our country he first ploughs the land and then sows the seed. The Jews did just the opposite. First the Jewish farmer sowed the seed. He

A plough

"broadcast" the seed by hand, carrying it in a basket or in the fold of his tunic, scattering it a handful at a time. The plough, pulled by oxen or ass, was pressed down by the farmer, to push seed into the furrow. The seed spread far and wide. It fell on the path which the country folk had trodden hard and it fell among the thorns. The farmer threw seed there deliberately for both the path and the thorns were going to be ploughed up.

Jesus described this in his parable. It was a real-life story about all the enemies of the farmer in getting a harvest. Jesus often spoke of himself as gathering in God's harvest. The disciples were beginning to think that their labour was useless—it seemed to bear little fruit. Jesus told them to learn a lesson from the farmer. Like him they must be confident that a harvest would come. Their labour was not in vain.

The early Christians often told this parable in their preaching. They added to the story of Jesus exactly what they thought every detail meant. Some of the seed fell on the path that the village folk had trodden across the field. The earth was pressed down and hard-baked by the sun. The birds made a free meal of it before ever the farmer could plough it. Some people's hearts were like that path—hard and obstinate. They too would bear no fruit. Jesus must have been thinking of the scribes and Pharisees with their hard hearts, their closed minds and their blind eyes. Nothing could grow in such hard and barren soil.

Some of the seed fell on stony ground. The soil was very thin in many parts of Palestine. Only a layer of earth covered the limestone rock beneath. Such soil was not deep enough for roots to form. The seed sprouted quickly and sprang up, but without good

MONTHS OF THE JEWISH YEAR

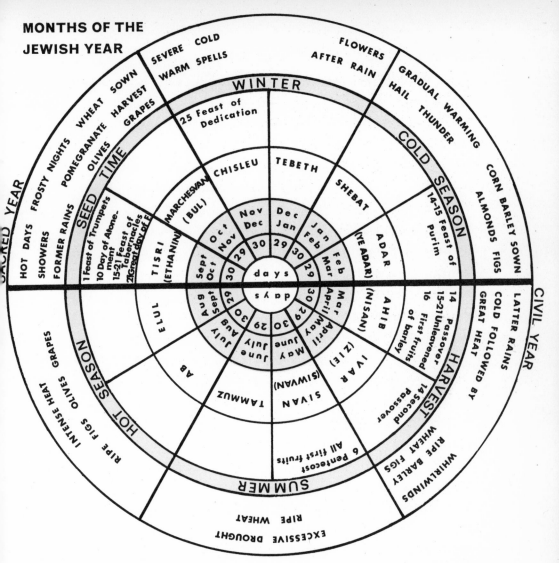

The year was based on the sun, but months on the moon. A month was from one new moon to the next. 12 lunar months were 354 days, but the year of the sun was 365 ¼ days. Every few years an extra month was added to the year to make up the difference—like our February 29 in a leap year.

In ancient times the Jewish year began naturally in the autumn when the crops were gathered in and the year of nature was ended. Later, Jews took over the civil or legal year of Babylon, which began in the spring.

That is why they still have two calendars—one religious and the other legal or civil.

roots and moisture it soon withered away. Some people were like that. We still call people "shallow" who have no depth and no roots. Jesus must have been thinking of the Galileans. They were easily roused and excited—revolts against the Romans often arose in Galilee. But they were shallow and fickle and their enthusiasm soon faded away. They flocked to Jesus, the new prophet, with his exciting teaching about the coming of God's kingdom and his wonderful powers of healing. But they soon found that he was not the kind of Messiah they wanted. He did not promise them wealth and ease; he would not do great wonders; he said nothing about driving out the Romans. They soon withered away.

Some of the seed fell among thorns. The thorns sprang up more quickly than the corn and soon choked it. The hearts of many who heard Jesus were choked by thorns, too. The poor peasants worried about lack of work and bad harvests, about getting clothes and shelter, about where the next meal was to come from. They were tempted to be dishonest, to rob and to steal. Jesus knew their hard lives and often thought of them. He was a peasant himself. He had no home, no money, not even a head-rest. He told them not to worry— God would provide for them just as he did for the birds.

The rich, too, were choked by worries, and Jesus knew how hard it was for their hearts to bear a harvest for God. Their cares were for thieves in the town and brigands on the road, for trading that must be profitable and for harvests that must be gathered in. How hard it was for a rich man to enter God's kingdom!

Some of the seed fell on good ground, soil that was clean and ready to receive it when the plough turned it in. It bore a rich harvest, more than making up for the seed which was wasted, as any farmer would realise. To the farmer in Palestine a tenfold return on the seed he had sown was a good harvest—an average harvest was a return of sevenfold or eightfold. But in the parable of Jesus the return was thirtyfold, sixtyfold and even one hundredfold! This was fantastic, but this was God at work. The harvest of the kingdom would be as bountiful. The disciples must be like sensible farmers who did not despair over seed that was wasted and labour that seemed in vain. In hearts which were ready to receive it, the kingdom would bear a rich harvest.

Jesus reminded his disciples of something else. All the prophets had sown the seed before them. They were reaping a harvest, too. "Have you forgotten the saying—'four months from seed-time to harvest'?" Jesus said to them. "Look around you. The fields are already white and ready for harvesting. The kingdom of God is already here. The harvest is ready to be gathered in."

Wheat and tares

There was something else which troubled the disciples of Jesus. Some of them had been disciples of John the Baptist. They remembered how stern John had been against evil. He had said that God was like a farmer at harvest time, separating the grain from the husks. The good grain would be gathered safely in and stored. The bad and useless husks would be burnt. Surely the kingdom of God was only for good people? Yet Jesus welcomed all kinds of people, no matter how bad they were. He was kind and tolerant to everyone—except to those who were proud of their goodness. Why was there so much evil among the people of God? Why did God allow it? How could his perfect kingdom come on earth among people like that?

Jesus answered these questions in the parable of the wheat and the tares, another story based on real life. A certain farmer, he said, decided to grow wheat in his field. He planted first-class seed, thoroughly tilled the ground to turn the seed in, levelled the soil and left it to grow the crop. But at dead of night an enemy of his crept into the field and scattered the seeds of a deadly weed all over it. This sounds a strange and wicked deed to us, but it was sometimes done in those days. The Romans even had to make a law against it. It still happens sometimes today in the East. For one of the worst things you could do to a man you hated, when you wanted revenge, was to ruin his harvest.

The deadly weed was called darnel, which is very similar to bearded wheat. Its seeds are very like wheat seeds except in colour. As it grows, it is impossible to tell darnel from wheat. Only when the heads appear on the stalks can they be distinguished—and then it may be too late. For the darnel roots intertwine with the roots of the wheat. That was why they had to be weeded out again and again as they grew and could be seen—a tedious job often done by the women of the household. But in the story of Jesus there was so much darnel that weeding out would have ruined the crop. The best thing to do, the master of the house decided, was to let them both grow till harvest time. Then, as the reapers cut the crop with their sickles, they could gather the grain into sheaves. The darnel could be gathered up later and tied in bundles to dry. Then it would be useful as fuel for the fire.

God's world is like that field. Good and bad people are mixed up together. The farmer certainly did not like the weeds growing in his field, but he had to be patient and to put up with them till harvest time. God is patient, too. There were good and bad among his chosen people, but the disciples must not start trying to separate

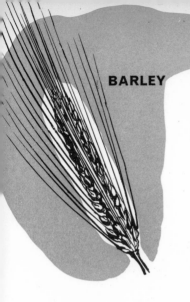

BARLEY

Barley was used by poor village folk for making bread (John 6.9,13). Rich people in towns had bread made of wheat. Barley was also used for feeding cattle and donkeys, for oats were rare. The rabbis called it 'animal food'. Barley was sown after the October rains. Harvest came in March-April. The country romance told in the Book of Ruth concerned barley harvest at Bethlehem (Ruth 1.22).

Wheat cost twice as much as barley. It was the most precious of all cereals, and the main food. It was harvested about a month later than barley. The Plain of Jezreel was famed for growing wheat. In the time of King Solomon there was so much wheat that some was exported to Phoenicia.

WHEAT

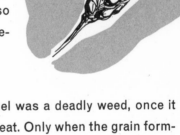

DARNEL

The bearded darnel was a deadly weed, once it got among the wheat. Only when the grain formed in the head could the weeds be distinguished from the wheat.

If the darnel seeds get into the grain used for making bread they cause a kind of poisoning, with sickness and drunkenness. That is why the French call this weed 'ivraie' ('ivresse' means drunkenness).

Pulling out the tares at harvest time was a dull and tedious job. Wives and children usually did it.

them. Only God knows men's hearts; only he could know. In his own good time, when the seed had had plenty of time to ripen, he would judge. Christian disciples must not be like the sect of the Pharisees, or the monks called Essenes who lived apart in the wilderness—or even like John the Baptist and his followers. Each of these groups separated themselves and claimed to be the true people of God. They alone were holy and pure, they thought. Christians must not be like that. The kingdom must be preached and the harvest must have time to grow. The disciples must be patient and leave the rest to God.

The fig tree

If you had lived in Palestine in the time of Jesus the three most common things you would have seen in the countryside would be vines and olive trees and fig trees. Fig trees needed more moisture than olives and grew better on higher land. Sometimes they were grown in groups, but you would often have seen a single fig tree in a small vineyard or beside a house. Fig trees grew to a great age and they produced fine crops if they were well looked after. They grew as high as 40 feet. Their branches spread far and wide and were covered with big thick leaves—like palm leaves. That is why Adam and Eve, in the story of the Garden of Eden, are said to have made aprons of fig leaves. Fig trees gave fine shade from the sun, especially when vines trailed through their branches, making a thick, shady covering. It was very pleasant, during the heat of the day, to sit peacefully under your own fig tree with its trailing vine.

Fig trees are mentioned over fifty times in the Bible, and naturally they appear in the parables of Jesus. In one of them he spoke of the fig tree as the herald of summer. The fig tree was different from

82

THE FIG TREE

A fig tree that was well cared for produced its fruit for ten months of the year. There were three crops: (1) The main crop called 'late' or 'autumn' figs, from August up to winter. They grew on the new wood. (2) 'Green' or 'winter' figs which did not ripen and stayed on the branches through winter. They were eaten when the wind blew them down. (3) 'Early' or 'first-ripe' figs, best of all for flavour. They remained on the tree and ripened in June. The Bible speaks of all three crops: (1) Jeremiah 8.13 and 29.17; (2) Song of Solomon 2.13; (3) Isaiah 28.4; Jeremiah 24.2.

Jesus once looked for fruit on a fig-tree at Bethany when he was hungry (Mark 11. 12-14). It was not the season for either late, autumn figs or early, first-ripe figs.

He expected to find green or winter figs, for the tree had plenty of leaves, but the tree had no fruit at all. This too was a parable of the Jewish people—full of religion but bearing no fruit of faith and goodness.

other trees, like the olive, for it shed its leaves. All winter it seemed dead with its spiky twigs and bare branches. Then suddenly, in February or March, it burst into life again as the rising sap burst into buds, and leaves followed in April or May. No wonder the fig tree was the first sign of summer.

Jesus mentioned other weather signs, too. A cloud rising in the west meant rain. A south wind—the sirocco wind from the Sahara desert—meant hot weather. "You are very clever at telling what the weather will be," Jesus said to the Jews. "You can read the signs and know what they mean. You can read the signs of nature, too. You know that summer is near when leaves appear on the fig tree. But you cannot read the signs of the kingdom of God in my words and deeds. If you were not so blind you would have recognised that his kingdom has long been in bud. Now it is in leaf and God's summer is at hand. What hypocrites you are!"

Since the fig tree was so common the Jews made many sayings about it. Once Jesus said, "Men do not gather figs off a thistle bush, do they? Of course not. Figs only come from a fig tree. You recognise the tree by its fruits. In the same way you know a good man by his good deeds, and an evil man by his evil deeds. You must beware of false prophets, of hypocrites whose lives do not match up to their words."

The fig tree was often used as a symbol, too. Like the vine it stood for the Jewish people. Jesus told a parable about a man who planted a fig tree in his vineyard. When the crop was due he went to

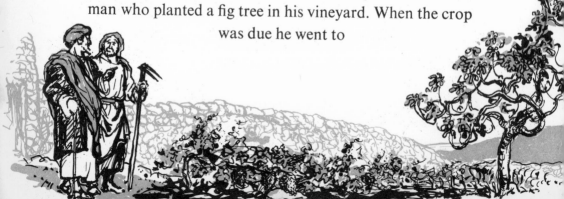

gather it. He was angry when he found no fruit on it. "This is the third year running that I have found no figs on this tree," he said to the man who looked after his vineyard. "Cut the wretched thing down—I can't waste good ground on a useless tree!" But his vine-dresser said, "Why not give it just one more chance, sir. Leave it for one more year. I'll dig round it and manure it. We might well get a crop next year if I nurse it. If we don't, then we'll definitely get rid of it."

The crowd knew that Jesus was speaking of the Jewish people. They were like the barren fig tree. God had nurtured his people for long centuries. He had sent them prophets, so that they might bear fruits of faith and goodness, but they were barren. Now God had sent his son. It was their last chance. Would they heed him, enter into the kingdom of faith and goodness, and bear fruit at last?

The vineyard

Many of Jesus' parables were like that. They were full of a sense of crisis. His teaching was urgent. There was not a moment to lose, for at last the kingdom of God had come on earth. The Jews had to choose. If they cast out Jesus and rejected God's kingdom it would be given to other peoples of the earth. They must make up their minds—quickly!

Jesus made that very clear in the parable of the vineyard. He told it during that last week in Jerusalem, when the leaders of the Jews were already plotting against him. His story was about a vineyard owned by a foreigner. There were many foreigners among the mixed population of Galilee. Some of them grew rich and bought up large estates. They went off to live in the city or to travel abroad. Sometimes they left stewards in charge, as we shall see. Sometimes they let their fields and vineyards to tenants. The contract laid down that an agreed rent was to be paid each year at harvest time. For in the ancient world rent was usually paid in produce, rather than in money.

In the parable of Jesus the landlord went off and sent his trusted agents each year at grape harvest to collect the rent. His tenants were very disgruntled men. They bitterly resented paying rent to the greedy landlord. He was rich, they were poor. Why should he have a fat share of their harvest for doing nothing? They rebelled. When the landlord's agent turned up the first time they beat him up and threw him out of the vineyard empty-handed. The landlord sent another. The wicked husbandmen had grown bolder. They stoned him to death. When the landlord heard what had happened he realised how serious it was. "Enough of this! I'll send my son," he decided. "Those rascals knew they were only dealing with slaves. It'll be a very different matter when my son arrives. They won't dare play him up. He'll soon make them toe the line and pay my rent." So the landlord sent his son. But when the tenants saw him coming they said, "Here's our chance! Kill him and the vineyard is ours for keeps!" They murdered the landlord's son and cast his body outside the vineyard.

That was not the end of the parable. Jesus often ended a story with a question to make his listeners think. Then they would have to decide for themselves what it meant and how it applied to them. "What do you think that landlord will do now?" he asked the scribes and Pharisees and priests who were listening to him, hoping to catch him out. "Naturally he'll see justice done to those wicked tenants. He'll ask for government troops to restore law and order, to punish those murderers, and to restore his property to him. Then he'll find new tenants."

The sting of this parable lay in its ending. The religious leaders in the crowd were furious with Jesus. They knew perfectly well what it meant. The vineyard was the Jewish people. The landlord was God. The agents were the prophets. They themselves were the wicked tenants. And, to add to this, this prophet of Galilee was saying that he was the son of God! They would have seized him there and then if it hadn't been for the crowd who hung on Jesus' words. They went away angrily to plot how they could arrest this Galilean and get rid of him.

The parable was a true life story of Galilee in those days. The Romans had cruelly put down a revolt there in A.D. 6, but there was still much unrest. The people of Galilee seethed with discontent at their poverty, the hard times, and the hated Romans with all their tax demands. The Jews of the south felt much the same. Jesus foresaw what must happen. It came in A.D. 66 with the final revolt against Rome, and the long and bitter war which ended with the destruction of Jerusalem in A.D. 70.

A VINEYARD

Palestine was much more fertile in Bible times than in modern times, for the soil has been eroded. Vines grew plentifully. Tradition said that Noah planted the first vineyard after the Flood (Genesis 9.20). When Moses sent spies into Canaan they came back with huge clusters of grapes (Numbers 13.23). In Isaiah 5.1-2 we read how a vineyard was made. A hillside was chosen; terraces were made on it, with a wall or hedge to enclose it. The ground was dug with a mattock and cleared of stones.

The vine was left to grow freely along the ground, or held up by props. Or it was planted among fruit trees so that it could trail from tree to tree. Hence the description of peace as a time when 'every man shall sit under his vine and under his fig tree' (Micah 4.4). The only work needed was to keep the wall in repair, to pull up weeds, to prune so as to get good fruit, and to water when necessary.

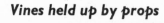

Vines held up by props

A WATCH-TOWER

Every vineyard included a watch-tower. It was built as a shelter for the man guarding the vineyard from thieves, from jackals, and from 'the little foxes that spoil the vines' (Song of Solomon 2.15). It was called also a 'booth' or 'tabernacle'. It was made of stones, about ten or more feet high. Brushwood or branches were used, fixed on posts, to provide shelter from the sun by day and dew by night. Sometimes the whole family slept here during the harvest season or even for the whole summer. The inside was a store-house. Stones jutting out of the cone-shaped tower acted as a staircase for climbing to the top.

Read Isaiah 5.2; Matthew 21.33; 1 Chronicles 27. 25; Isaiah 21.5 and 8.

Jackal-scare

A jackal-scare was simply a pile of white-washed stones set up in the vineyard to scare away these very common dog-like animals.

Labourers in the vineyard

Unemployment was another cause of unrest in Galilee in the time of Jesus. This was the background of another parable he spoke about a vineyard. It concerned the grape harvest, which lasted from August to September. At the end of September the rainy season began, and all the grapes had to be gathered in before the rains started. Every day mattered. The owner of a large vineyard hired every man he could get to pick the grapes before it was too late. The working day was from 6 a.m. to 6. p.m. in our time—the Jews went simply by the sun. That was why, in the parable, the owner of the vineyard went to the market-place at dawn to hire men for the day. The best workmen were there, waiting to bargain for a good wage. They agreed to work for a denarius—a silver Roman coin which was the most common money in Palestine in the time of Jesus. It was a good day's pay for a labourer, and these workmen went off cheerfully to the vineyard to begin the long day's work.

Time was so short and the work so urgent that the employer went back to the market-place throughout the day—about 9 a.m., again at noon and again about 3 p.m. He hired every man he could get. These men were glad to get work—they trusted their employer to give them a fair wage for the hours they put in. He even went back again at 5 p.m., when there was only one hour left of the working day, for it was a race against time now to gather and press the grapes. There were still men loitering and gossiping in the market-place. "Why do you lounge around here all day doing nothing?" the employer chided them. "We're unemployed," they said. "Hurry into my vineyard and get to work," the owner replied. "There's still an hour left." Off they went, relying simply on their employer's generosity.

When work ended for the day it was the steward's job to pay the workmen. "Give all of them a full day's wage," his master ordered. "Start with those I took on last." Imagine the delight of those last workmen when they each received a denarius—a full day's wage and a good one at that. Then came the workers hired during the day. They each received a denarius, too—much more than they had dared to hope for. Last of all came the men who had done a full day's work. They had bargained for a denarius: they each received a denarius. They were angry. After all, the other workers had been paid so handsomely that they naturally expected more than they had bargained for. They began to grumble, shaking their fists in the direction of the employer's house. They even went up to the house, dragging the other workmen with them. The master came out and the ring-leader shouted angrily at him, without even the usual courteous address. "We've slaved a full twelve hours in your vineyard all through the heat of the day!" he shouted. "These lay-abouts here have worked for only one hour in the cool of the evening. Yet you've paid us no more than them!" The employer addressed him courteously. "My dear sir, you seem to think I'm cheating you. Didn't you agree with me to work for a denarius? I decided to pay these others the same as you. What are you complaining about—my generosity? Can't I do what I like with my own money? If I choose to pay these men the same as you that's my business, not yours. Are you envious because I am generous? Take your wages and be off with you."

What a topsy-turvy story that was! No employer, then or now, could hope to run a business successfully in that kind of way. But the parable was not a lesson in business and in money-making. It was a lesson on the kingdom of God. It was teaching about God

THE JEWISH DAY

The legal day was from sunset to sunset (not our midnight to midnight). The natural day was from dawn to sunset, that is, the hours of daylight. This working day was about 12 hours (John 11.9). It was sometimes called 'dawn-dusk'.

OUR TIME	JEWISH TIME	BIBLE REFERENCES
6 a.m. 7 a.m. 8 a.m. 9 a.m.	THIRD HOUR	Labourers hired for the day's work (Matthew 20.1). Jesus was crucified during the third hour (Mark 15.25).
10 a.m. 11 a.m. NOON	SIXTH HOUR	Jesus sat by the well of Samaria about the sixth hour (John 4.6.).
1 p.m. 2 p.m. 3 p.m.	NINTH HOUR	The nobleman's son was healed at the seventh hour (John 4.52-53). Jesus died on the cross in the ninth hour (Matthew 27.45-50).
4 p.m. 5 p.m. 6 p.m.	TWELFTH HOUR	The last labourers hired at the eleventh hour i.e. nearer 6 p.m. than 3 p.m. (Matthew 20.6-7). End of the day's work (Matthew 20.8).

People in the East did not worry about exact time as we do. The day was divided into four general periods: the exact hour did not matter. The length of hour varied from 49 to 71 minutes according to the season of the year and the hours of daylight. The division of the day into hours was invented in Babylon, and was brought to Palestine by the Greeks and Romans. The Jews did not bother about exact hours, let alone minutes and seconds.

THE JEWISH NIGHT

It was the Roman night of 4 watches each of 3 hours.

BIBLE REFERENCES	JEWISH TIME	OUR TIME
FIRST WATCH Mark 13.35	EVENING	6 p.m. to 9 p.m.
SECOND WATCH Mark 13.35	MIDNIGHT	9 p.m. to Midnight
THIRD WATCH Peter denied Jesus during cockcrow (Matthew 26. 34 and 74-75). Mark 13.35	COCKCROW	Midnight to 3 a.m.
FOURTH WATCH Jesus came to his disciples on the Sea of Galilee (Mark 6.48). Mark 13.35	DAWN	3 a.m. to 6 a.m.

From earliest times the night was divided into 'watches' which a soldier kept on guard duty or a shepherd with his flock. In Old Testament times the night was divided into three 'watches' (Psalm 63.6 and Psalm 90.4)—first watch, middle watch and morning watch (Luke 12.38). But they were not precise times.

By the time of Jesus the Jews had copied the Roman division of the night—4 watches of 3 hours each (Mark 13.35).

The Jews were even more vague about night hours than about daytime hours. In any case, the hours of night varied in length, too. On December 25, the winter solstice, there were less than 9 hours of daylight. Then the day hour was only 45 minutes and the night hour was 75 minutes. In summer it was just the reverse.

A ROMAN SUNDIAL OF THE TIME OF JESUS

The sundial was invented in Athens, and it was used by Greeks everywhere in New Testament times. The water-clock, another way of telling the time, was invented in Alexandria. It was more precise than the sundial. Some water-clocks were very ingenious. At each hour they threw a pebble up into the air. Others made a whistling noise.

We do not know whether Jews used either of these ancient clocks. The Bible does not mention them at all, except for two possible references to sundials (2 Kings 20.11 and Isaiah 38.8). Rich Jews would probably have some kind of clock in their houses, just as the Greeks and Romans in Palestine did. Jewish peasants would simply go by the sun.

The Roman sundial seen here had a pointer fixed in the slot where the lines meet. It stuck out horizontally and the shadow it made showed the hour. When the sun was low in winter, the hour was shown on the top semi-circle. The middle circle showed the hours in spring and autumn. The bottom rim showed the hours in summer from the shadow cast when the sun was high. All the year round, therefore, this sundial indicated a day of twelve hours.

94

and his generosity. The owner of the vineyard was a generous man. He knew that unemployed men had hungry wives and children. In fact, their needs were greater than those of good workmen who got regular work. It wasn't their fault if they were unemployed. The employer deliberately paid them first to show what he thought. If he had paid first those who had worked all day they would have gone home quite content. There would never have been any trouble.

The parable turned the way of the world upside down. But so does the kingdom of God. God is like a father who gives to his children according to their need—not according to what they have earned. "Think how generous he is," Jesus said. "He does not pick and choose; he has no favourites. His rain falls on the fields of evil men as well as on the fields of good men. His sun ripens the crops of bad men as well as the crops of pious men."

The owner of the vineyard was God; the workers were men of different kinds. Some, like the Pharisees, thought they could bargain with God. Because they kept every detail of God's sacred Law they thought this made them righteous in His sight. It was as if God kept an account book and recorded all their religious acts. When they were added up it was clear that God owed them a reward. No wonder they were so proud and looked down on ordinary folk and sneered at sinners. Their religion was bargaining with God. They got what they bargained for, and no more. But other men, like those workers taken on during the day, simply trust in God's goodness. And many, like those taken on for the last hour, rely only on his generosity. Such trust is richly rewarded by God.

Jesus told this parable to answer a question from Peter. "We have given up everything to follow you," Peter said. "What reward will God give us?" The parable taught him not to think of rewards, not to bargain with God. God does not need the service of men. He takes them into his vineyard only out of the goodness of his heart. Trust in him. He is far more generous than we can possibly imagine.

A rich farmer

Not all landowners were as wise and good as the owner of that vineyard, as another parable shows. One day a man in the crowd said to Jesus, "My elder brother has taken two-thirds of our father's money. Tell him to share it equally with me." By Jewish law that was quite right. The eldest son always inherited two-thirds of the father's estate so that the family would go on. Jesus answered the greedy man sternly. "Who appointed me to settle your family affairs?" he said. Then he turned to the crowd and said, "Beware of greediness. A man's value depends on what he is—not on what he has." Jesus explained what he meant by a parable of a rich and foolish farmer.

A certain farmer, he said, owned a lot of land. He had built up his estate by his own hard work, and by skilful farming over the years he produced fine harvests. Now that he was rich he had to decide what to do. He thought of no one but himself. He decided to pull down his barns and granaries and build much bigger ones to store all his produce. "Now I can retire," he said to himself, gleefully. "I've worked hard all these years. Now I'll sit back and enjoy myself. Nothing to worry about—I've got enough put by to last me for years. I'll have a really good time for the rest of my life—eating and drinking and merry-making." But that night God spoke to him, "You foolish man. Death will come to you this very night.

Now who will enjoy all the wealth you have stored up for yourself?"

This was a parable of selfishness. The farmer was not being punished by God for his greediness. Death comes to everyone sooner or later. Jesus was showing the folly of living only for earthly things. There is nothing wrong with money or wealth; it is love of money that is foolish. "Your heart will be where your treasure is," Jesus said. "Have your treasure in heaven. Then your heart will be in the right place."

When a man dies people say, "What was he worth?" They mean, "How much money did he collect during his life?" To God money is worth nothing; in his eyes the rich farmer possessed nothing. "Why," said Jesus, "a man could own the whole world and still be worth nothing to God." The rich farmer had wasted his life. Only a selfish fool lives for money.

Finding treasure

Many Jews in Palestine were like the rich farmer and kept their wealth in goods. Others kept it in the form of precious stones. Money only attracted robbers. There were Jewish bankers in the time of Jesus, but most people did not keep their money in banks as we do. Those who had money hid it for safety. In the newspaper today you may read of an old person being robbed of money that was kept in a tea-pot or under the bed. The Jews kept money in the ground. There was a Jewish proverb which said, "The safest place for money is the earth." A man dug a hole in the ground and hid his money in it. Now only he knew where it was. It was safe there from robbers in time of peace, and from soldiers in time of war. Sometimes a man might bury his money and then go away and never come back. He might die or be killed in a distant place. Then his money still lay hidden in the earth. If someone found a buried treasure it was his. According to Jewish law, finding was keeping.

Jesus told a story of a man who did just that. Walking across a derelict field, one day, he stumbled against something hard in the ground. Curiosity made him bend down and scratch at the earth to discover what it was. Imagine his delight when he found it was a buried treasure. Hastily he covered it up again. He went into town and found out the price of that field. Then he sold everything he had—lock, stock and barrel—to raise the money. Everything he possessed went to buy that field. But it was more than worth it to own that treasure.

It is like that, Jesus said, with the kingdom of God. A man may come across the kingdom of God by accident. But, once he has found it and realised its value, he will gladly give up everything to gain it. He knows it is the greatest treasure of all.

Another man, said Jesus, kept his wealth in pearls. Pearls were as valuable in the East as they are with us today. In fact they were doubly valuable for men loved them for their sheer beauty. Happy the man who could own a beautiful pearl to give him daily delight! The man in the parable already owned some pearls, but he was always on the look-out for a more lovely gem. One day in his travels he found it—the most exquisite pearl he had ever seen. He could not rest content till he possessed it. He threw caution to the winds. He sold his pearls, sold his house, sold his lands—he sold everything he had in the world to get that pearl. It was more than worth it to own that treasure.

Some people do not stumble across the kingdom of God by accident. They have to search hard for it. But when at last they find it they at once realise its value. They give up everything to gain the finest treasure of all. The kingdom of God is costly, it demands sacrifice. But the man who gains it knows that it is worth more than everything he owns.

The fisherman

Though many of the people of Galilee lived by the harvest of the land, many others lived by the harvest of the sea. A lot of Galileans were employed in the fishing industry around the Sea of Galilee. Fish was one of the main foods of the people of Palestine. Fishermen sold their produce all over the land, and they had a large export industry as well.

Fishermen used three kinds of nets. By far the biggest was the draw net or drag net. A group of men worked together with it. Some rowed the fishing boat out off-shore taking the drag net. They lowered the net into the sea, for it was heavy with floats at the top and weights at the bottom. Then the net made a wall in the water, cutting off the fish between it and the shore. Other men on land pulled hard on the ropes, drawing the net slowly towards the beach. Others held up the sides of the net, throwing stones to prevent any fish escaping. Now every fish in the water between the net and the shore was imprisoned. At last the net was safely hauled up on the beach, with its huge, mixed catch. Now all the fishermen sat down and sorted it. Much of the catch was useless and was thrown back into the sea. But the rest was valuable and it was carefully packed in baskets.

Jesus likened his work to fishing. The men he had called to help him were to be "fishers of men". The parable of the drag net described their work. Like fishermen, they had to cast their net far and wide to draw men into the kingdom of God. The net contained a very mixed catch. A lot of it was useless—fish that could not be eaten, seaweed, stones, and bits of driftwood. The catch had to be sorted out.

The kingdom of God was just like the drag net, bringing in a mixed catch of men. They had to be sorted, too, for not all were worthy. Even among the twelve apostles there was one who denied Jesus and another who betrayed him. But the kingdom must be offered to all men; the net must be cast far and wide.

THE DRAG NET

This kind of net is sometimes called a 'seine' (from the Greek word for it, 'sagene'). It was as big as 500 yards long, and 12 feet deep. It was best worked from two boats, as in another Gospel story (Luke 5.1.-11). The huge net was lowered carefully from the fishing boat in a wide semi-circle and then drawn slowly to land. The nets were very costly and they needed regular repairs. For drying in the sun they were hung from trees or bushes, or spread out over the boats. Fisherman worked in teams for drag net fishing, and were partners in the business. Simon Peter was the leader of such a group.

The shepherd

Rearing sheep was another common way of earning a living in Palestine. All through the Bible we read about sheep and shepherds, and naturally they come into the parables of Jesus, too. Sheep were kept mainly on the limestone hills of Judaea where the soil was too thin for agriculture but did give rough grazing for the animals. Bethlehem was a centre of the sheep industry, with shepherd villages in the hills around it. Some shepherds were still nomads, but most lived in settled homes in the countryside.

Sheep were kept in Galilee, too. Rich men employed shepherds to look after their flocks. Shepherding was a hard life. The shepherd had to be out in all weathers, enduring the fierce heat of the day and the bitter cold of night. By day he had to be on constant watch, guarding his sheep from rocky precipices, from vicious thorns, from venomous snakes, and from beasts of prey. He had to lead them to green pastures and to still waters, caring especially for ewes giving birth and for little lambs. By night he guarded them with his own life, lying across the door of the fold to keep out crafty thieves and stealthy beasts. He was paid usually with milk or wool, sometimes with sheep. His was a hard and lonely life with only his dog for company, if he had one.

Many countrymen had small flocks, looked after by their children or by relatives. Sheep were kept for wool rather than for meat, so that they were kept for a long time. Each one was known to its owner, and each one was precious. "Suppose," said Jesus, "that a man had a hundred sheep. If one was missing, when the flock came back to the fold, you know what he would do. He would leave the ninety-nine safe in the fold and go to search for that one lost sheep. He would risk his life in the darkness in order to find it.

102

He might lose his foothold on an unseen precipice; he might be attacked by wild beasts; he might be bitten by a snake or wounded by piercing thorns. He would not think of that—he would listen intently for the frightened bleat of his little lamb. He would go on until he found it. How happy he would be when at last he discovered it! He would lay it on his shoulders tenderly and carry it back home with great joy. He would be so excited that he would cry out to his neighbours and friends, 'Come and celebrate with me! I've found my lost sheep!' I tell you, it is just like that in heaven when a lost sinner comes back home to God. There is more joy in heaven over one single sinner who repents than over ninety-nine good men who do not need to repent."

SHEEP FOLD

Sheep folds were made in the hills for guarding flocks at night. Their dry-stone walls were made as high as possible and covered with thorn bushes. Beasts of prey were many in Bible times —hyenas, jackals, wolves, and even bears and lions. If the shepherd was alone, he lay across the entrance to the fold so that no beast could reach them; he himself was the door (John 10. 7-11). Sometimes several shepherds arranged to meet at the same fold for the night. Then one kept watch while the others got some rest. Some folds even had watch-towers, like those made in vineyards, to keep a look out for thieves or beasts of prey.

THE SHEPHERD'S TOOLS

Rod

This was a club, about 3 feet long, made from an oak sapling or from a tree root. Sometimes flint or metal was fixed on the end to drive off beasts of prey. It usually hung by a strap from the shepherd's wrist.

Staff

Every Jewish traveller carried a staff mainly for defence against enemies and dogs. 'To have no staff' was a saying which meant 'very poor' (Matthew 10.10; Mark 6.8). It was about 6 feet long. A shepherd needed one most of all. His had a curve on the end for taking hold of a sheep by its leg or its body. It was his crook. It is symbolised today in the 'pastoral staff' of a bishop.

Horn

The shepherd carried olive oil in a horn. It was used to treat the wounds of sheep when they were bitten or scratched or hurt.

Sling

The sling was made of a leather thong, or of plaited rushes or hair or animal sinews. The centre was widened and hollowed out to take a smooth round stone. It was twirled round the head and, when one end was suddenly let go, the stone flew to its target. Shepherds practised with it daily and were deadly accurate. They used a sling to defend their flocks or to warn a sheep going astray or lagging behind. Many armies had slingers in ancient times, too.

Jesus spoke this parable to religious people like the Pharisees. They were shocked again and again at the way Jesus behaved. Any decent rabbi would spend his time gravely discussing the sacred Law with other devout men. But not this prophet. He spent his time with the riff-raff of the town—with traitor tax-collectors, with sinful men and with bad women. He hobnobbed with them in the streets, went into their homes, even sat at table with them eating and drinking. The company he kept was a positive scandal and an absolute disgrace to all decent, religious people.

The Pharisees told Jesus exactly what they thought about his carrying on. He answered them in this parable of the lost sheep. "God does not need to worry about good men like you," Jesus said, with irony. "After all, it's sick people who need the doctor, not folk who are bursting with good health. You despise these people and condemn them. I care for them because God cares for them, each and every one. The safe home-coming of one lost sheep gives him much more joy than all you good men who are safely in the fold. I did not come to call good men into the kingdom of God. I came to seek and to save those who are lost."

Sheep and goats
Goats were as common as sheep in Palestine. The nimble mountain goats could go much higher than sheep and they could live on rougher grazing. Goats were also reared by the Jews. Often they were mixed together with the sheep and they were only separated for feeding and milking and herding. Even a peasant family would have a goat. Rich men had hundreds. Goats had many uses. Like sheep, they were used for sacrifices. They could give as much as six pints of milk a day. The milk was used for making butter and

THE GOAT OF PALESTINE

The goat was a cheap animal, much less valuable than sheep. But it had many uses and was valuable to the peasant for its milk, hair, skin (for making bottles) and horns. A goat would only be killed for a feast or a party (Luke 15.29), though it was used as a sacrifice (Leviticus 4.22-26; Hebrews 9.13-14). There are still wild goats (the ibex, with horns three feet long) on the hills of Palestine. The name Engedi, an Israeli settlement by the Dead Sea, means 'Well of the wild goat'. Goats are still valuable domestic animals, too.

Goats, being much more active, always led a mixed flock of sheep and goats (Jeremiah 50.8). They were frisky and much less obedient than sheep. When a shepherd separated sheep from goats there was no doubt as to which were more valuable.

cheese, as well as for drinking. Goat hair was woven to make clothes and tent-cloth, and it was also used for filling mattresses. Bottles and rough garments were made from goat skin. Goat meat was eaten, and even goat horns were useful for containing oil.

Male goats kept apart, but female goats often mixed with the ewes in one flock. They could easily be distinguished and separated for the goats were black and the sheep were white. Jesus told a parable about this. When the flock came to the fold the shepherd laid his staff across the entrance. He let the sheep pass in, but he lowered his staff to turn the goats away. It will be like that, Jesus said, at the end of the world. Men will be assembled before the throne of God and he will judge them. He will separate the sheep from the goats, putting the sheep on his right hand and the goats on his left. To the sheep on his right hand he will say, "Come, enter into your inheritance. The blessedness of my kingdom is for you. For when I was hungry you fed me; when I was thirsty you gave me drink. When I was a stranger you took me in; when I was naked you gave me clothes. When I was ill in bed you came to see me; when I was shut up in prison you came to visit me." These chosen ones will be amazed. "But Lord," they will say, "when did we do all this?" God will reply, "When you did these acts of love to your fellowmen, to the very least of them, you did them to me. For they are my brothers."

To the goats on his left hand God will say, "Depart from me. When I was hungry or thirsty you gave me nothing. You never took me into your homes or gave me raiment. You never visited me when I was ill or in prison. It is for these things that you are rejected." They too will be amazed. "But Lord," they will say, "when did we we fail you? If only we had recognised you we would of course have done all these things and more." God will reply, "When you failed to do these acts of love to your fellowmen, to the very least of them, you failed to do them to me. For they are my brothers."

There were many Jewish stories like this, about God's judgement in the life to come. They spoke of men being cast out by God, of souls being condemned and punished and burnt in everlasting fire. The first Christians were all Jews. Scholars think that details from these Jewish stories were added on to the parable of Jesus. His simple parable was one of the most beautiful of all. It teaches that we can only show our love for God by showing love to our fellowmen. It has inspired Christian men and women all down the ages to care for the humble and the poor and the needy simply for love of Jesus.

Travelling

Our last parable of country life is a story about travellers. We know it as the parable of the Good Samaritan, one of the most famous parables of all.

Once the Jews had ended their desert wanderings and settled in the promised land they did as little travelling as possible. There were still some who were desert nomads, moving with their flocks and herds from one oasis to another, but most Jews lived in towns or villages and seldom went far, except on pilgrimage to Jerusalem. They loathed the sea, and even on land they never travelled for pleasure. In any case, travelling was dangerous. Jews on a journey always went together in a caravan if they possibly could. The leader and guide was called "the eye of the caravan". Most people walked, but some rode on donkeys. Few ordinary folk had a camel, and only courtiers and soldiers had horses. The main Roman roads were first-class. Other roads were merely tracks or paths.

To travel alone was asking for trouble—most of all on the desolate road from Jerusalem to Jericho. It winds through wild and barren hills, with caves and boulders offering fine hiding places for brigands. It was always a dangerous road. In the time of Jesus it was called "the red road" for so much blood was shed there. The Romans built a fort on it to protect travellers. In the Middle Ages the Crusaders had to protect pilgrims who used it on their way to the Holy City. Even in modern times bandits have made it dangerous. The road drops 3,000 feet in its 20 miles from high Jerusalem to low-lying Jericho. That is why Jesus began his parable, "A certain Jew went down from Jerusalem to Jericho and fell among thieves." Everyone knew what he was talking about, especially his disciples, for they had just come along that road with Jesus on his last journey to Jerusalem.

The robbers beat up the traveller and made off with everything he had, even his clothes. They left him half-dead. As he lay there three men came hurrying along the road, one after the other. The first was a priest from Jerusalem—a man whose whole life was given to God and spent in his service. He saw the Jew lying there, but he hurried by on the other side of the path. A little later came a Levite —one of the servants of the priests in the temple at Jerusalem, men looked up to by common folk for their religious lives. He too hurried by on the other side of the path.

Jesus does not say anything against these two men of religion. They were not bad men—they were just useless. But they had lots

110

ROMAN MILESTONES IN PALESTINE

The Jews, not being great travellers, did not build proper roads. Nor did they have wheeled transport which would need roads. A rough 'way' between one place and another was good enough for travellers on foot or on asses. The most they did was to level the ground, fill in holes and remove stones (Isaiah 40.4 and 62.10). In bad weather such 'ways' would be useless.

The Romans were very different. The movement of troops and the control of their empire depended upon their fine, permanent roads. Their roads were carefully built, layer on layer, and raised for good drainage, or made of blocks of limestone carefully cut and cemented together. They also built fine bridges. The main Roman roads were in Syria, north of Palestine, and to the east of the river Jordan. These Roman milestones, which still stand today, are by the road in the Arnon valley, east of the Dead Sea. When a Roman emperor built or repaired a main road he always set up new milestones with his own inscriptions on them. That is why two or more milestones stood next to each other, as in this picture.

There were Roman roads in Palestine, west of the river Jordan, but they were not so carefully made as they were not needed for troop movements or for communications.

of excuses for not stopping to help their fellow-countryman. For one thing he might be dead, and to touch a dead body defiled a Jew. It meant going through long religious ceremonies of washing to be purified and fit again to take part in the worship of God. For another thing the robbers might still be lurking around—it was dangerous to linger. There were other good reasons, too, for hurrying by. The priest and Levite lived strictly by the sacred Law of God, keeping every detail of it. It said nothing about helping wounded men. Again, Jews believed that suffering was sent by God. It was his judgement on a sinful man. If the Jew lying in the road was being punished by God they must not interfere. They had lots of good excuses.

The third man who came along was a Samaritan traveller. The people of Samaria were hated by the Jews. Samaritans were half-breed Jews who worshipped the same God and lived by the same Law, but the Jews regarded them as foreigners and pagans. They even prayed against them in their synagogues, and certainly had nothing to do with them if they could possibly avoid it. Samaria lay between Galilee in the north and Judaea in the south. A good Jew travelling between north and south always took the long route round by the river Jordan to avoid going through the territory of the Samaritans. Things had got even worse in the time of Jesus. One night, when he was a boy, Samaritans had crept into the Temple at Jerusalem during the great Passover Feast. They had thrown the bones of dead men around the court of the Temple so as to defile it. The crowd of Jews must have bristled when Jesus brought a Samaritan into his story.

Worse was to come. This Samaritan was the hero of it! For he was so full of sympathy for the poor Jew that he at once got off his donkey to help him. He used his own olive oil to bathe the Jew's wounds, and his own wine to stop the bleeding and to quench the poor man's thirst. He tore up his own garment to make bandages and to bind up the injured man's wounds. He risked his own life, too, lingering there on the lonely road. He lifted the Jew on to his donkey, supporting him there, till they reached the only inn on the road. The Samaritan was a regular visitor there. He used his own money to pay the innkeeper to look after the Jew, giving him two silver denarii. As he left, he promised to pay the innkeeper more on his next trip if that was not enough. The only thing that mattered to him was that the poor Jew should be cared for and made well again.

Jesus told this parable to a scribe—one of the teachers of the sacred Law. Jesus had agreed with the scribe that the two greatest commandments were to love God and to love one's neighbour. The Jews took this to mean a fellow-Jew, certainly not a foreigner. But the scribe asked Jesus about this—"Who exactly is my neighbour?" he said. After Jesus had told him this parable he asked him a question—"Which of these three men was neighbour to the wounded Jew, do you think?" "Why, the one who showed loving-kindness to him, of course," answered the scribe. "You have answered your own question," Jesus replied. "Go and do likewise."

Jesus did not condemn the useless priest and the useless Levite. It was their religion that was wrong. It forbade them to touch a man who might be dead. Besides, they may have been hurrying to Jerusalem for the Temple service. To them it was much more important to serve God in his house than to serve the wounded man in his need. Jesus was teaching something quite new. Jews believed that foreigners were outside God's love. Jesus believed that God's love

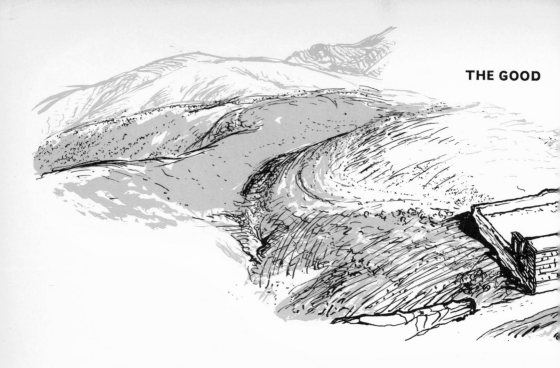

The building on this spot today (shown above) is Turkish, but it is on the site of much older ruins. It may well have been here that the inn stood which Jesus passed on his way from Jericho to Jerusalem, and which he referred to in his parable. For inns were few and far between. Hospitality has always been very important in the East, and a man could usually find somewhere to stay. The inns which did exist were nothing like our hotels. Travellers always

SAMARITAN INN

carried their own food and drink and bedding. The inn was simply a square with a wall round it. Wealthy travellers hired one of the few small rooms. Others laid out their beds under the wooden gallery while the animals were tethered in the open courtyard. If there was an innkeeper, you had to pay him for any attention you wanted from him.

has no limits. Jews lived by the letter of the Law, by what it said. Jesus lived by the spirit of the Law, by what it intended. Jesus was teaching that your neighbour is anyone who needs you, anyone you can help. A Christian's love must be like God's love. It must have no limits.

"Tiberius Caesar, son of the divine Augustus"

"Augustus: Chief Pontiff (high priest of Roman religion)"

A ROMAN SILVER DENARIUS

The denarius is the Roman coin from which we got our 'd' in 'l.s.d.'. It was one of the commonest coins in Palestine in the time of Jesus. The Roman mints made coins of gold or silver. Subject kings were only allowed to make coins of bronze. The silver denarius was the coin that had to be used for paying Roman taxes. It was worth about 9d, but money had a much greater value then. It was the daily wage of a workman (Matthew 20.2), and it would be a good day's keep for a man staying at an inn (Luke 10.35).

You can find other references to the denarius in—Matthew 22.19; Matthew 18.28; Mark 6.37; Mark 14.5; Luke 7.41; Revelation 6.6.

References for parables in this chapter

Seed growing secretly	Mark 4.26-29; compare Matthew 9.37-8.
The mustard seed	Matthew 13.31-2.
The sower	Mark 4.1-9; compare John 4.35-38.
Wheat and tares	Matthew 13.24-30.
The fig tree and weather signs	Luke 13.6-9; Mark 13.28-31; Luke 12.54-56.
The vineyard	Luke 20.9-18.
Labourers in the vineyard	Matthew 20.1-16.
A rich farmer	Luke 12.16-21; Mark 8.36-7.
Finding treasure	Matthew 13.44 and 45-46.
The drag net	Matthew 13.47-48.
The lost sheep	Luke 15.3-7; Mark 2.17.
Sheep and goats	Matthew 25.31-46.
The good Samaritan	Luke 10.25-37.

Seed and sower

Make your own chart of the year of nature in Palestine.

Jesus said, "A mustard seed of faith can move mountains" (Matthew 17.20). What do you think he meant by this? Write a story to illustrate this. You could choose a man or woman in history whose faith was able to "move mountains". Or you can make up your own story.

You can bring the parable of the sower to life by growing seeds, mustard and cress if you like, in a flat box. Divide it into four parts for good earth, stony earth, hard earth, and earth with other seeds in it. Then you can watch how they grow.

Write a modern parable of the sower. You will need to describe different kinds of adults, or boys and girls, and what harvest of good each kind produces.

Draw the parable of the sower in a series of picture as a strip cartoon.

Act the parable of the wheat and the tares, using your own words.

The fig tree
Look up these references to fig trees in the Bible:
Judges 9.7-15; 1 Kings 4.25; John 1.48; Genesis 3.7; 2 Kings 20.7; Jeremiah 24.1-3; Nahum 3.12; Matthew 7.16. Use reference books, too, to write an account of the fig tree in the Bible.

The vineyard
There are two parables here to act—the wicked husbandmen, and the labourers in the vineyard. Use your own words in your acting. Make a model of a vineyard of Palestine. As well as the vines it will need a fence or wall around it, a watch tower, jackal scares, and a fig tree too.

You can read another parable of a vineyard in Isaiah 5.1-7. In what ways is this like a parable of Jesus?

Read the parable of the labourers in the vineyard together in dramatic reading, as if it were a play. You will need a 'narrator' to read the background of the story, and readers for each of the speaking parts.

Find out if your local museum has a Roman denarius, or can borrow one for you to examine. Draw this coin, or model it in plasticene or alabastine, or make a rubbing of it.

A Rich Farmer

Read and learn by heart the saying of Jesus in Matthew 6.19-21. Read also 1 Timothy 6.10.

Read this parable in dramatic reading, like a play. You will need a narrator, to read the background of the story, and two other readers for the rich farmer and the voice of God.

Make up a prayer from this parable. It will be about unselfishness and having our treasure in heaven.

Finding treasure

Act or mime these two parables of treasure in the field and the pearl of great price.

Write a newspaper article to explain the Jewish proverb: "The safest place for money is the earth".

Among the Jews, finding was keeping. To us this is quite wrong, Can you think why we should be different from the Jews in this?

The shepherd

Read these Bible accounts of the shepherd—Psalm 23; Psalm 80.1-5; Isaiah 40.11; Ezekiel 34.7-31; John 10.2-18. Use reference books, too, to write a newspaper article on shepherding in Palestine. Model or draw the shepherd's tools.

Draw the parable of the lost sheep in a series of pictures as a strip cartoon.

Letter Psalm 23, the shepherd's psalm, in illuminated writing if you can. Make sure you know it by heart. Find and read together hymns in your hymnbook which speak of God as our shepherd. Learn a new one to use in School Assembly.

Sheep and goats

Use reference books to write a newspaper article on goats in Palestine.

Imagine you were a Jewish boy or girl in Palestine in those days. Describe your family's goat and tell of all the things which come from a goat.

In what ways can we put into practice the teaching of this parable? After you have talked about this, make up a story of a boy or girl who showed love for God by deeds of love to others.

Write the story of a man or woman, either in history or today, whose life illustrates this parable.

Travelling

Act or mime the parable of the Good Samaritan.

Draw this parable in a series of pictures as a strip cartoon.

"Neighbour" really means "nigh-dweller"—one who lives nigh or near you. What does it mean to a Christian? After you have talked about it answer this question in your notebook.

In what ways can we be "Good Samaritans" today?

THE SHEPHERD'S MUSIC

Double pipe

Jewish boys could easily make pipes from reeds to play with—for example, to play at weddings or funerals in the market-place (Matthew 11.16-17). Shepherd boys had plenty of time on their own, when they were out with the flock, and playing the flute was a common pastime. A single pipe was quite enough. But a number of pipes was bound together to make a double pipe, or even more to make a mouth organ.

Single pipe

Early mouth organ

Another popular musical instrument was the lyre. David the shepherd boy played skilfully on it (1 Samuel 16.23). One kind of lyre was the 'kinnor'. It was made of wood and for strings twisted grass or sheep gut was used. Another kind was the 'nebel'. It was bottle-shaped and it was made from the shell of a tortoise and covered with animal skin; it had five strings fixed to a crossbar. Simple harps or lyres could be easily carried about and played walking or sitting.

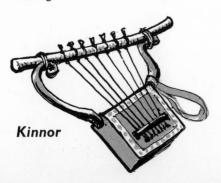

Kinnor

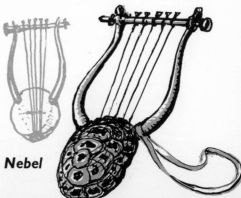

Nebel

The fisherman

Draw or model the three kinds of nets used by fishermen in Palestine.

A group of fishermen using the drag net would be a fine subject for a painting. Or you could draw their work in a series of pictures as a strip cartoon.

General

Write in your notebook a description of (1) A Scribe; (2) A Levite; (3) A Pharisee. Reference books will help you.

Imagine you were the son or daughter of one of the countrymen in Palestine described in this chapter, choosing the one that interests you most. Write an account of your father's work and illustrate it with your own drawings.

Make up a story of country life in Palestine in the time of Jesus. It can be about any of the different people described in this chapter.

All the class can help make a wall-frieze of country life in Palestine. It will need pictures, paintings and drawings, as well as descriptions of all the different kinds of country people.

OTHER WAYS OF FISHING

(See Habakkuk 1.15)

A cast net This net was draped on the fisherman's arm as he stood in shallow water near the shore. It was whirled round and thrown on to the water in a cone. Weights made it sink and trap the fish from above. The fisherman pulled it to shore or dived down, held the bottom of the net to contain the fish and then drew it in. After the catch was sorted, the nets had to be cleaned, mended and hung up to dry (Matthew 4.18-20).

Spearing fish

This was done at night, using torches, held over the stern of the boat, to attract the fish. When they came towards the light they were speared with a harpoon or trident (Job 41.7).

Hook and Line

Sometimes hook and line were used by a fisherman standing on the shore. Jesus suggested this to Peter when they needed money to pay the temple tax (Matthew 17.27).

PALESTINE IN THE TIME OF CHRIST

~~~~ Roads

Dion cities of the Decapolis

Mediterranean Sea

TYRE

PHOENICIA

Mt. Carmel

CAESAREA

GALILEE

Mt. Hermon

to Damascus

Dan

Caesarea Philippi

Chorazin

Capernaum

Bethsaida

Sea of Galilee

Raph

Magdala

Cana

Tiberias

Hippos

Dion

Nazareth

Gadara

Nain

Scythopolis

Pella

SAMARIA

Samaria (Sebaste)

Shechem

Gerasa

Arimathea

Joppa

Ephraim

Philadelphia

Jericho

Emmaus

JERUSALEM

Qumran

Bethany

Bethlehem

Gaza

to Egypt

Hebron

Dead Sea

Machaerus

JUDAEA

NABATAEA

Masada

Beer-sheba

IDUMEA

Miles

0   15   3

walled city

citadel

open city

Town Life

Cities, towns and villages

In the Old Testament we often read of wars and fighting in Palestine. That was why people needed to live together and to be able to defend themselves and their homes. They lived in strong cities which could be defended. A city would have a citadel, or strong place, inside it and thick walls all around it—sometimes a moat and ramparts as well. People who lived in the countryside round about would take refuge in the city as soon as danger threatened. But they had to pay taxes to the city for this. Such a city was called "mother" and the villages round about were called its "daughters". Cities such as Jericho, Jerusalem and Samaria were tiny compared with our cities today. The streets were narrow and the houses were tightly packed. This was partly to keep out the heat of the sun, but it was also because there was so little room inside the walls. Streets were not paved and they were very dirty. Refuse was thrown out into the streets and the wild dogs scavenged among the rubbish.

As times became more settled, towns grew up. They had no defences. They were usually market towns for farmers and traders. They were crowded, too, with houses and courtyards and crooked streets all jumbled up together. Towns that Jesus knew were Nazareth and Capernaum and Nain. The Romans gave certain rights to towns—for example, in administering justice.

Villages in the time of Jesus had no such rights. They were

125

simply groups of small houses or huts huddled together. Villages Jesus knew were Bethphage, Bethany and Emmaus.

Sometimes a village grew up for men with the same occupation. There were shepherd villages around Bethlehem. Towns grew up in this way, too. Sepphoris in Galilee grew out of a village of weavers, for this was where flax grew. In the cities and towns it was common for men of the same trade to live in the same street. They formed a kind of trade guild or trade union. In Jerusalem there was a Street of Bakers, a Street of Butchers, and a Street of Smiths. In Nazareth there was a Street of Carpenters and a Street of Weavers. City gates were named after the trade which used them most and for which they were made. Jerusalem had a Sheep Gate and a Fish Gate, for example.

AN ALLEY IN OLD NAZARETH TODAY

This was the kind of street Jesus would have known in the towns of Palestine.

126

Cities and towns and villages were given names which had a meaning. Many began with BETH, a Hebrew word meaning HOUSE. BETHPHAGE means HOUSE OF FIGS; BETHSAIDA means HOUSE OF FISHERS; BETHLEHEM means HOUSE OF BREAD; BETHEL means HOUSE OF GOD. The name of SAMARIA, a city built on a fine hill, means PLACE OF WATCH. JERUSALEM means CITY OF PEACE.

Towns were busy, noisy places. Noisiest of all was the market-place which was the open ground just outside the city gates. Everything took place here: farmers sold their produce; traders shouted their wares; law cases were tried here in the open air; travellers brought news from afar; town meetings were held; business deals were made, with much haggling; children ran in and out playing their games; townsfolk chatted with their friends, exchanging news and gossip. Some of the townsfolk went out to work in the fields during the day. But many were tradesmen such as bakers, butchers, barbers and hairdressers, fullers or laundry-men, dyers, water-carriers. Others, such as goldsmiths and makers of scents and perfumes, provided for the luxuries of the wealthy townsmen.

Jesus had grown up in the town of Nazareth. He made the town of Capernaum his headquarters for his ministry in Galilee. He often visited the city of Jerusalem for the great religious feasts. He knew all about the bustling life of the towns and the people who lived in them. Many of his parables were about town life. They give us a vivid and real-life picture of the towns of Palestine during his life on earth.

Children in the market-place

We will begin with the children. It was like Jesus to mention them for he knew and loved them well. He loved them for themselves and sometimes sat with them on his knee with his arms about them. He loved them for their nearness to God, and he spoke of the angels of God watching over them. He loved them for their trust and their humbleness, and he drew lessons from them for his disciples. When he was teaching men about prayer he said, "If your son wants a small loaf to eat, do you give him a stone? Or if he asks for fish, do you give him a snake? Of course you don't. You sinful men give your children good things. How much more, then, will your heavenly Father give good things to those who ask him! Ask for what you need in prayer. You will find how good and generous he is."

Jesus knew the games which the children played in the market-place. Like all children they imitated grown-ups. They would play mothers and fathers, doctors and patients. Playing at weddings and funerals was most popular of all. The boys played on pipes while the girls sang, or wailed as they danced. But, of course, there were tiffs and sulks and tears. Jesus spoke of these when he was talking to the Jews. "You are like children, sitting in the market-place, playing tunes on their pipes for the others to act a wedding or a funeral. 'It's not fair', they call out to the others. 'When we play a wedding jig you won't dance. When we pipe a lament you won't wail and beat your breasts!'" This was the boys quarrelling with the girls. For, among the Jews, the men danced at weddings, and it was the women's task to mourn at funerals. The boys and girls were accusing each other of being spoil-sports.

"You Jews are just as silly and childish," Jesus said. "John the

128

THE MARKET-PLACE

Baptist came out of the desert. His life was as stern and harsh as his teaching. What did you say about him? 'He's a raving lunatic, a wild man of the desert—he can't be a genuine prophet!' you said. Then I came, sharing in the life of ordinary folk in their homes and villages and towns. And what do you say about me? 'He's a glutton and a wine-lover, mixing with the riff-raff of the town—he can't be a genuine prophet!' you say. You're never satisfied, are you. You can always find something to object to, something to quarrel with. How blind you are! John came, heralding the kingdom of God. I come, bringing God's kingdom among you. And all you can do is to find fault and to haggle like children at play."

129

The unforgiving servant

Kings and rulers, of course, lived in towns. Naturally they appear in the parables of Jesus.

Simon Peter was a big, bluff, hot-tempered man. He often got angry with his brother Andrew. Once he came up to Jesus in a temper and said, "How often do I have to forgive this brother of mine? Until seven times?" Now Peter knew what the rabbis taught about forgiveness. Men should really be as forgiving as God is. But they are only human. The rabbis thought that to forgive three times was as much as could be expected. Peter knew that this would not be enough for Jesus. That was why he increased it to seven times. Surely that would be enough. But Jesus replied, "Not seven times, Peter. Seventy times seven." This was a typical Jewish way of speaking. It did not mean 490 times. It meant, "You should forgive without limit, just as God does." Jesus told a parable to explain forgiveness.

A JEWISH PRIEST

There was once a great emperor who ruled over many lands. He appointed officers called satraps to govern his lands, to keep order and to collect taxes for him. They were mighty men, but they only kept their power at the emperor's pleasure. He decided to see if they were being faithful and loyal to him. All the satraps were summoned to the imperial palace for their accounts to be examined. This had not been done for a long time. It turned out that one of these governors owed the emperor 10,000 talents. It was a huge, impossible debt that the satrap had built up, over the years, by cheating the emperor of his taxes. It was in fact fifty times more than the Roman taxes for the whole of Galilee and the land across Jordan in one year! Jesus deliberately chose the most valuable currency known to the Jews, and the highest number they used in counting, in order to make the debt huge and impossible.

The emperor was furious. He ordered the proud satrap to be sold into slavery, and his wife and children too. Among the Jews a wife could not be sold, but in other lands this was common. Everything the satrap owned must be sold. The proceeds would not pay off much of the debt, of course. But the emperor was so angry that he could only think of punishing the rascally governor. The satrap tried to save himself. He threw himself, grovelling, at the emperor's feet. "Have patience, lord", he wept. "I'll pay back every penny I owe you." He was very human—somehow he'd find the money, he imagined. Of course the emperor knew that he couldn't. But he was full of pity for the governor. He did not rebuke him for his folly. He did not condemn him for his greed and dishonesty. He simply forgave him the whole, huge, impossible debt.

The governor went out of the palace trembling with relief. Phew! What a fate, and he had only missed it by a stroke of luck! And what a fool he had been to land himself in such a mess! Then, suddenly, he noticed one of his minor officials. The rascal owed him a hundred denarii, didn't he? It was scoundrels like him who got a man into debt! Still smarting from his humiliation the governor rushed up to him. "Pay your debts!" he shouted, seizing him by the collar. He was quite within his rights, of course. For the law said that a debtor could be seized by the collar and dragged off to prison if he could not pay what he owed. The poor man threw himself, grovelling, at the governor's feet. "Have patience, lord," he wept, "I'll pay back every penny I owe you." His debt was only about £20 and, although he was a poor man, he could repay it— it was not like a huge, impossible debt of millions of pounds. But the governor had no pity. He had the man thrown into the debtors' prison.

The story of what had happened soon spread. The other servants of the emperor were shocked and horrified. The news soon reached the emperor's ears and he sent for the governor. "You wicked scoundrel!" he cried. "I forgave you your huge debt when you implored me. But you could not forgive your fellow-servant a tiny debt when he implored you. Very well! I'll treat you exactly as you treated him! You can go to debtors' prison, too. But you'll be under the torturers till you have repaid every penny you owe me!" To punish a man by torture was forbidden among the Jews. But it was a common punishment in other lands. And, since the governor could never repay his huge debt, his punishment would last for the rest of his life.

This was a parable about God's judgement at the end of time. "That is how God will treat you," Jesus said, "if you do not forgive each other with all your hearts." We owe God a huge, impossible debt. He forgives us freely and endlessly. Debts owed to us by others are tiny by comparison. We must forgive them as God forgives us. A hard, unforgiving heart separates us from him. Our forgiveness depends upon our forgivingness.

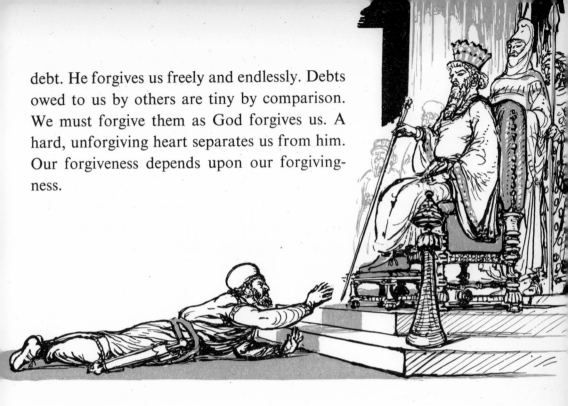

Two foolish rulers

Two short parables of Jesus about rulers were, like others, based upon real-life happenings.

Jesus was speaking about the kingdom of God. He often spoke of it as God's gift. But that did not mean that it was easy to accept it. To enter God's kingdom demands sacrifice. Evil things must be given up—and sometimes things that are not evil in themselves. "Count the cost before you decide," Jesus said. "Suppose, for example, a man is going to build a tower. First, he sits down and plans it and counts the cost. If he does not work out his costs, you know what will happen. He will get halfway through his building and then have to abandon it for lack of funds. How everyone will mock him and laugh at him for his folly!"

133

Everyone knew whom Jesus was referring to. Pontius Pilate, the Roman Governor of Judaea, had decided to build an aqueduct. It was to bring water to Jerusalem from the reservoirs at Bethlehem, seven miles away. The Jews were very angry because he took money from the Temple treasury to help pay for it. But they were delighted when Pilate ran out of money and had to abandon the work. How they mocked him and laughed at him for his folly!

Jesus gave another example. "Suppose a king is going to war," he said. "First, he must sit down and plan his campaign according to the size of his army. He has to decide whether he can risk meeting the enemy's army of 20,000 men when he has only 10,000 men. If he does not consider carefully, before he sets off, you know what will happen. Before his army even sights the enemy host he realises that he is heading for disaster. Hurriedly he sends envoys to the enemy to do him homage and to surrender."

That was almost exactly what had happened to Herod Antipas, the ruler of Galilee. He had married the daughter of Aretas, an Arab chieftain. Then he married his own niece named Herodias. This was against Jewish law and John the Baptist was shut up in prison for saying so. It also caused trouble with Aretas whose daughter had been rejected. Herod went on a campaign against him. But he had not planned his campaign and he was badly defeated. Like Pilate, he had not counted the cost.

A Roman Aqueduct

SECTION

RESERVOIRS AT BETHLEHEM

It was from the reservoirs at Bethlehem that Pilate built his aqueduct to carry water to Jerusalem. There are three at Bethlehem, the biggest being nearly 600 feet long. They were called Solomon's Pools, for the first cisterns here dated back to his time.

The Romans were good engineers. They repaired these reservoirs. They are three miles south of Bethlehem.

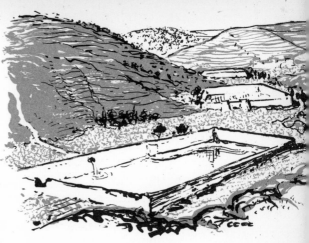

Pipe

Wise Men's Well

PILATE'S AQUEDUCT

Pilate's aqueduct must have run for 10 miles in all. Part of the distance it was carried in pipes made of stone drums set in a concrete wall. Part of Pilate's aqueduct is still used at this well on the road between Bethlehem and Jerusalem. This is the traditional Well of the Wise Men, for it is said that they used it. The shepherd or goatherd draws water from the well and pours it into this stone 'cup' for the animals to drink out of. It is this stone cup that came from Pilate's aqueduct.

A selfish rich man

In the towns Jesus met Pharisees and Sadducees—especially in Jerusalem. The Pharisees were pious laymen who lived strictly by the Law. The Sadducees were the priestly party who, unlike the Pharisees, had no belief in life after death. They were powerful, rich, and worldly, and they kept well in with the Romans so as not to lose their power. Pharisees and Sadducees were wealthy men of standing. They were looked up to as men of God by the common people, they were respected and feared.

Both Pharisees and Sadducees wanted to know more about this new prophet from Galilee. Who did he claim to be? The Messiah of God? If he was a genuine prophet let him give them a sign, perform some wonder, do something miraculous. One day a Sadducee asked Jesus for such a sign. Jesus answered him in a parable. It was about a selfish rich man. We call him "Dives"—the Roman word for "a rich man". The story shows that he had no belief in life after death. For him death was the end. Clearly Jesus was describing a Sadducee in his story of Dives.

Dives lived in a fine mansion. He enjoyed all the good things of life—rich food, costly wines, comfort and luxury and ease. His was an idle life—not for him the commandment "six days shalt thou labour". Nor did the other commandments bother him much. Since death was the end he might as well enjoy this life as much as possible. He was selfish and self-indulgent. He wore pure and costly purple robes, like pagan kings. But then, he lived like a king and like a pagan, too. Even his underclothes were made of the finest linen from Egypt.

Now a certain lame beggar lay every day outside the gate of the rich man's mansion. His name was Lazarus which means "God is my help". It was a good name, for he was a devout man who loved God. He lived on the tit-bits left over from the banquets which Dives had. Jews ate with their hands, not with knives and forks. After dipping their fingers in the dish they wiped them on pieces of bread and threw the bread under the table. When the servants cleaned up after meals they threw these bits of bread out into the street. Lazarus shared them with the scavenger dogs of the streets. They lurked around him, gobbling greedily. They even licked the sores on his wasted body.

DOGS

The Jews did not keep dogs as pets, as we do. Some shepherd dogs were imported from abroad. Palestine dogs, often mentioned in the Bible, were scavengers of the streets. They were very like jackals, and had tails like wolf-dogs. They were short-haired and tawny in colour. They were always hungry, for no one wasted food on dogs. They roamed the streets, snarling and yapping, and howled by night (Psalm 59.6). They lived on any rubbish or filth they found in the streets.

137

Precious purple dye was made from the gland of a sea snail called the murex. It was only found along the coast of Phoenicia. The dye made a rich red-blue colour which was known as 'royal purple'. For only very rich men and rulers could afford robes dyed with this precious purple.

FINE PURPLE

Persian and Roman rulers wore purple.
The veil of Solomon's temple was made from it, and
the high priest's garments were decorated with it. Jesus
likened the 'lilies of the field' to King Solomon's robes
because they were purple in colour (Matthew 6.28-29).

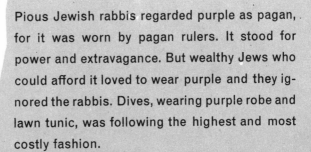

Pious Jewish rabbis regarded purple as pagan,
for it was worn by pagan rulers. It stood for
power and extravagance. But wealthy Jews who
could afford it loved to wear purple and they ignored the rabbis. Dives, wearing purple robe and
lawn tunic, was following the highest and most
costly fashion.

At last the sufferings of Lazarus were ended by death. His body was thrown into a pauper's grave. No one grieved or mourned for him—he was only a common beggar. But the angels of God carried his spirit up to heaven—"Abraham's bosom", as the Jews called it. There at last he knew comfort and ease and honour for he was placed at the right hand of Father Abraham himself, the seat of the most honoured guest.

Not long afterwards Dives himself died. He was given a splendid and costly burial—as befitted so wealthy and important a man. But his selfish spirit was not fit for the blessedness of heaven. He found himself in the abode of departed spirits which the Jews called SHEOL and the Greeks called HADES. There was torment for Dives there. But the worst torment was to be able to see the blessed ones reclining in bliss. For the Jews believed that heaven and Sheol were close to each other, even though there was a gulf between them which none could cross. Dives could see the beggar, who had once lain at his gate, reclining in honour in the bosom of Abraham.

This was a very popular story among the Jews. It had come from Egypt where it was very common, too. The Jews made the rich man a tax-collector and the poor man a scholar. Everyone liked a story in which the rich and evil man had to change places with the poor

140

and good man in the life after death. Jesus used this popular story. But he added something new to it.

The Jews believed that the spirits of evil men abode in Sheol for about a year. During that time they could repent of their sins. Then, at the end of that time, Abraham would come and bear them up to heaven. Dives knew that there was no hope yet of Abraham coming to deliver him. But at least he could appeal for help, for he was a Jew by birth and Abraham was the father of all Jews. "Father Abraham," he cried, "have mercy on me! Send Lazarus to bring me water, for I am suffering terribly in this flame of torment." Dives

**THE HEBREW
UNIVERSE**

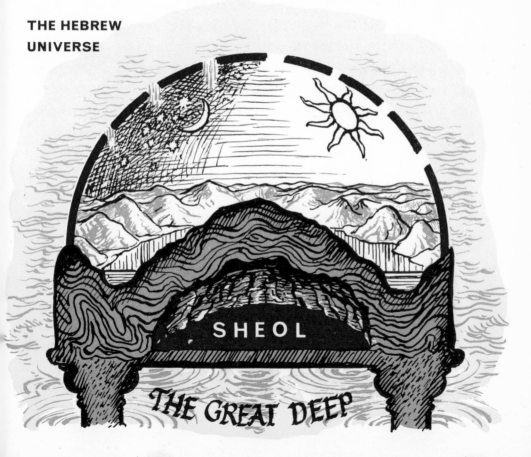

SHEOL

THE GREAT DEEP

had not changed one bit. He still regarded Lazarus as a worthless beggar—a slave to serve him. He had much to learn. "As a Jew you are my son," Abraham replied. "But you did not live as my son. You lived on earth in selfish ease, ignoring the Commandments. Lazarus lived in poverty and squalor, but he was a true son of Israel. Now he is rewarded and dwells in peace. You are rewarded with the torment you have earned. And the gulf between you is impassable." Then Dives cried out, "Father Abraham, if you cannot help me, at least send Lazarus to my five brothers on earth. He could warn them to change their lives so that they do not come to this place of torment." Abraham replied, "God has made himself known to them through the Law and the Prophets. Let them heed the Scriptures." "They need more than that," Dives cried. "If one who had died appeared to them they would believe and change their lives." Abraham answered him sternly, "If they take no notice of the Law and the Prophets they certainly won't be convinced by someone rising from the dead."

That was the answer of Jesus to the Sadducee who asked for a sign. If the sacred writings meant nothing to such men a miracle would be useless. The greatest wonder of all would be for God to raise someone from the dead. But God had already made himself known in the Scriptures. They were quite enough for anyone whose heart was really open to God. Those who asked for a further sign merely showed how far they were from God. Even the greatest wonder of all would mean nothing to such men. That was why Jesus would give no sign to convince such ungodly men.

We must always remember that a parable teaches only one truth. It would be quite wrong to think that Jesus was teaching about heaven and hell in this parable. He naturally used the ideas of the

142

Jews of his day. This parable was teaching about giving a sign—not about life after death. It was also a fine parable against selfishness.

The unjust judge

Every Jewish town had its law-court. The laws came from Jewish religion and they were carefully laid down. Rules for the courts were carefully worked out, too. But neither was much use if the judge was not a good man. Judges were strictly chosen. They would be older men, looked up to for their piety and wisdom. They were not paid. Hearing cases was a way of serving both God and man, without thought of reward. But money did come into it. Even if the judge could not be bribed, the court officials could. A rich man would always get his case heard quickly by bribes. A poor man could only wait. A rich man would get the verdict, too, if the judge himself were an unjust man. Jesus told a parable about just such a judge. Those who were innocent but poor did not stand much chance of getting justice from him.

It was even worse for a widow. Her life was very hard, in any case, for she had no one to support her. When her husband died all his estate went to the eldest son. She only received her wedding dowry. She had to wear special clothes—"widow's weeds", in the old English phrase—so that everyone knew her position. Her life was even worse if she had children and no relatives to help her. There were of course laws to protect widows, but any rascal could get round them. That is why the Bible often says that caring for widows and orphans is a sign of true religion. Without a man to provide for her and to protect her, and without money to bribe and to pay her way, a widow was helpless. Anyone could cheat her and get away with it—even in the law-court.

In a certain town there was an unjust judge, Jesus said. A poor widow came to court. She was being cheated out of money by a rich and powerful man. She had to seek justice herself, as the custom was—no one else would do it for her. But she had no money to bribe the court officials to get her case heard—let alone to bribe the evil judge. The rich man's bribe would have won him the case, anyway. Her only hope was to be persistent—to wear the judge down by leaving him no peace. Every day she was back again at the court. "Give me justice!" she kept crying out. "This man is cheating me!" She was a perpetual nuisance and in the end the judge could stand no more. "I'm not afraid of God or of men", he said to himself, "let alone widows. But really this is too much. I never get a day's peace from this wretched widow. I can't stand any more of it. There's only one thing to do to stop her pestering me—give her what she wants." So, simply by her persistence, the poor widow at last got justice.

Jesus himself showed what this parable meant. The poor widow finally got a hearing simply by pestering the hard-hearted judge. How much more, then, will God be ready to hear the poor when they cry to him! He listens patiently, ever ready to hear the cry of the humble poor and needy. He is a God of love, full of sympathy and tenderness. Day and night he will hear their cry and answer their pleas. Swiftly and suddenly he will give them the justice for which they yearn.

The Pharisee and the Tax-collector

The parables of Jesus often turned things upside down. For God's judgement is so different from men's judgement.

It happened, said Jesus, that two men went to the Temple for the service. There was one service at 9 a.m. and another at 3 p.m. One of the men was a pious Pharisee who lived strictly by the Law. That made him right with God. Like some Pharisees he was proud of his own fine character and his good deeds. He did not really need God. He trusted in himself and in his own goodness. He strode into the Temple as if he owned it. He stood alone out in the open where everyone could see him. He stretched out his arms and raised both his hands and his eyes up to heaven. He spoke his prayer, as the custom was. "God," he said proudly, "I must thank you that I am not like other men. I am not a greedy man, I do not swindle, I do not live immorally. I'm certainly nothing like that tax-collector over there. I live strictly by the Law. Why, I even go beyond it. I fast on both Monday and Thursday every week. I give a tenth of every-thing I have to the church. I even tithe the herbs in my garden, and everything I buy—even though it has been tithed already. No one could be more religious than I am." The Pharisee knew that his good deeds were recorded in heaven. What a huge bank balance of goodness he had stored up with God!

As the Pharisee had noticed, the other man was a tax-collector. He was a traitor, collecting taxes for the Romans—and cheating his fellow Jews at the same time. People treated him as a thief and he had no rights as a citizen. Everyone despised him and pious men like the Pharisee would have nothing but contempt for him. He knew that he could not pray as the Pharisees did. He stood at a distance where he would not be seen by the congregation. He

TAX-COLLECTOR

followed the other Jewish attitude for prayer—head bowed and hands crossed on his breast—for he did not dare even to lift his eyes up towards heaven. He smote upon his sinful heart in his sorrow and despair at being so far from God. He had no hope of being forgiven. To repent would mean to give up his occupation and to repay all the people he had cheated. But he did not even know them all. Nor could he condemn his wife and children to starvation. His only hope, his only trust was in God's mercy. Softly he murmured the opening words of a psalm, "God, have mercy on me, sinner that I am, out of your great goodness." The psalm went on: "A humble and penitent heart, a broken spirit—these are the finest sacrifices. You will never despise them." Hopeless sinner that he was, the despairing tax-collector could only trust in God and throw himself on his mercy.

The ending of the parable shocked those who heard it. "It was the tax-collector who was forgiven by God, not the Pharisee," Jesus said. "He went to his home justified by God. For God's mercy has no limits, his love has no bounds. Those who trust in themselves are far from him. But those who trust only in him are close to his heart."

No wonder this story shocked people. What wrong had the Pharisee done to be rejected by God? What good had the tax-collector done to win forgiveness? Nothing at all. But God judges men, not by their outward actions, but by their hearts. He can enter into a broken heart. But in a hard heart there is no room for him.

Synagogue at Capernaum (3rd century A.D.)

Two debtors

Jesus was once invited to the house of a rich Pharisee named Simon who lived in Capernaum. It happened, it seems, on the sabbath day. Jesus had addressed the congregation in the synagogue. Only men and boys sat downstairs. Women and girls followed the service from the gallery above. Jesus had spoken of God's love and forgiveness—especially for outcasts and sinners. After the service Simon invited the prophet from Nazareth to eat at his house. It was praiseworthy to offer hospitality to a visiting preacher. Simon had even arranged a banquet, for his guests reclined on couches; at ordinary meals they simply sat on cushions. It was in honour of Jesus, for he might be a genuine prophet. That was just what Simon wanted to find out.

Simon was certainly curious to find out about Jesus, and the banquet honoured him. But Simon did not want to honour Jesus too much. He did not bother with the usual courtesies—water for washing his guest's dusty feet, a kiss of greeting, perfumed oil to freshen his hair and face. They went straight to the couches, grouped around low tables. This custom of reclining at special meals was a growing fashion among wealthy Jews. They copied it from the Greeks and Romans. The feet of the guests were stretched out behind them on their couches. Thus, anyone coming into the room stood at their feet. The room opened on to the courtyard so that servants could come in and pass among the guests.

During the meal a woman stole into the room unnoticed. She was a sinner—an immoral woman, or a woman married to an outcast. Thus, whichever was the case, she had no hope of God's forgiveness according to strict Jewish religion. But now everything was different for her. The words of Jesus in the synagogue had

149

touched her heart deeply. Now she knew that God loved her, sinner that she was, and that her sins were forgiven. She had crept into Simon's house to show her gratitude to the prophet Jesus. She had brought with her a costly alabaster flask of scented perfume. She wanted to anoint him with the perfume to show how thankful she was. But she was overcome when she stood behind Jesus, and her tears flowed down on to his feet. She was so shocked when she saw what she had done that she completely forgot herself and where she was. She fell on her knees beside him. She removed the covering from her head and untwined her long hair. She wiped away her tears from Jesus' feet with her tresses and anointed them with her perfume. For a married woman to untie her hair when other men were present was a terrible disgrace. Some rabbis said that a man could divorce his wife if she acted so shamefully. But the woman was conscious only of Jesus. She kissed his feet—the symbol of thankfulness to one who had saved your life. For Jesus had saved her from her past and given her a new life.

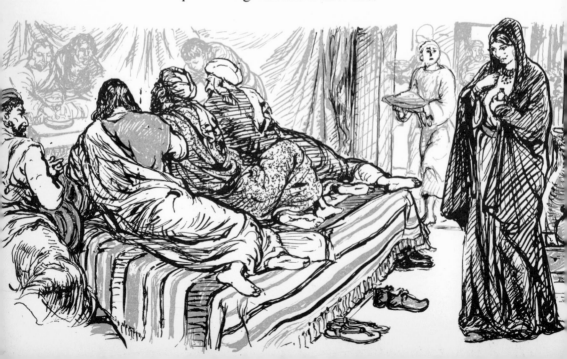

Simon and the other guests were shocked and disgusted at these goings-on. "If this man was a true prophet he would know what kind of woman she is," Simon murmured. Jesus read the Pharisee's thoughts. "Simon," he said, "I have something to tell you." "By all means," Simon politely replied. "There were two men who each owed a debt to a money-lender. One owed him fifty pounds: the other owed him five pounds. Neither of them could repay him. He forgave both of them their debts to him. Now—which of these two men will be the most grateful to him, do you think?" "The man who was forgiven most, I suppose," Simon replied. "Exactly," said Jesus. "You see this woman kneeling here at my feet? When I came to your house as a guest you offered me no water for my feet: but she has watered them with her tears and dried them with her hair. You gave me no kiss of greeting: but she has not ceased kissing my feet. You did not anoint my head with oil: but she has anointed my feet with her perfume. Her sins are many. But God must have forgiven them all since she is so full of love. One who has been forgiven little will have little love." Then Jesus spoke to the woman. "Your sins are forgiven. Go in peace."

This parable, too, turned everything upside down. The sinful woman was much closer to God, Jesus said, than the pious Pharisee. Her endless gratitude showed how much she loved God—and therefore how much she had been forgiven. Simon showed no such gratitude, for his love was small.

Feet washing

A guest's feet were hot and dusty from the road. His sandals were easily removed. His feet were washed by a slave of the household.

Kiss of Greeting

In the East it is natural to show one's feelings. Men kissed on both sides of the face. A host always greeted his guests with a kiss when they entered his house (e.g. Genesis 29.11 and 13) and again when they left (Acts 20.37).

Anointing with oil

Oil and perfumes were used by both men and women in the East. For they did not have soap to wash with, as we do, and the climate was very hot. Oil was freshening and scented the body. Anointing the head was part of everyday toilet (see Matthew 6.17).

A host always anointed the head of a guest on arrival at his house. It was a sign of happiness and joy.

Weddings

Jesus gladly shared in every part of people's lives. He went to the homes of rich people and of poor people, of religious men and of sinners. Naturally he went to weddings. He told parables about them, too.

Weddings were the happiest times of all for the Jews. They were very carefully prepared. First, the young couple were engaged by an arrangement between their fathers, and solemnly betrothed to each other. They made their promises to each other, and the bridegroom paid over an agreed sum, in money or in kind, to his bride and to her father. All this took place in the bride's house. The betrothal lasted for a year. To be betrothed was as binding as to be married. If the bridegroom died during that year the future bride was regarded as a widow.

At the end of the year of betrothal came the wedding celebrations. They lasted a whole week and usually took place in the autumn. Harvest was all gathered in and everyone could join in the festivities. The actual wedding feast was held in the evening at the bridegroom's house. He went with his friends, the "groomsmen", to fetch his bride. She waited for him at her house with her friends, the "bridesmaids". Each of the bridesmaids had a lamp, for their happy duty was to light up the joyful procession to the house of the bridegroom where the feast took place. Sometimes the lights for the procession were small copper vessels fixed on top of poles. Rags, soaked in oil, were burnt in these containers so as to make torches to light up the darkness of evening. Still today in India weddings are celebrated in the evening with torch-light processions like those of the ancient Jews. But among the peasants the lights were simply clay lamps with a wick burning in olive oil, just like those used in the home but with shades to protect the flame. The bride and bridesmaids never knew when the bridegroom and his groomsmen would arrive. Sometimes they had to wait for two or three hours. Sensible bridesmaids kept their lamps alight all the time, for it was not easy to light them quickly. And, of course, they carried extra oil with them in a container so that, if the bridegroom was late, they were in no danger of running out of oil. For it would be very shameful if their lights flickered out just when they were needed to light up the happy procession. While they waited they would gossip, or even doze if they were sleepy. But when the shouting told them that the bridegroom was approaching they had only to trim their lamps and they were all ready.

Bridesmaids

Now it happened at a certain wedding, Jesus said, that the bridegroom was delayed. The bride had ten bridesmaids waiting with her. Five of them were sensible girls, for they had brought some extra oil with them in case they had to wait. The other five were foolish, thoughtless girls who had brought no spare oil. They had to wait so long that they all fell asleep. Suddenly, about midnight, they were woken up with a start. "The bridegroom's coming!" was the happy cry. Hurriedly the sensible girls trimmed their lamps—filling them with oil and trimming the wicks. But by now the lamps of the five foolish girls were flickering low, for their oil was almost gone. "Share your oil with us!" they cried to the five sensible girls. "We dare not," they answered. "There would not be enough for us, and we must light up the procession. You had better go and buy some." The five thoughtless bridesmaids hurried off. Of course they were not back in time to join in the procession. While they were gone the

1

The bride dressed by her bridesmaids.
Read Isaiah 61.10; Jeremiah 2.32
and 4.30; Revelation 21.2.

2

The feast prepared in the bridegroom's
house.

5

The bridesmaids are woken and quickly
trim their lamps.

6

The whole procession, lit by the bridesmaids' lamps, goes to the house of the
bridegroom.

3

The bride waiting with her bridesmaids.

4

The bridegroom and groomsmen come to the house of the bride.

7

The wedding feast begins.

8

The door is barred and no one else can enter.

bride and bridegroom were escorted by their friends to the bridegroom's house where the wedding feast was all prepared. They all
went in, the door was shut, and the watchman stood on guard
inside. Soon afterwards the five foolish girls came hurrying back
and they banged on the door. "Lord! Open the door to us!" they
cried. But the bridegroom answered from within, "All my guests are
here and the feast has started. I will not have anything to do with
you!"

This too was a parable of the kingdom of God. Jesus proclaimed
God's kingdom and invited all to come into it. Some were wise and
prepared themselves for it. Others were thoughtless and careless
about it. But time was short—they risked being shut out from the
kingdom of God. Thus the oil was a symbol of repentance.

Later, Christians gave a new meaning to this parable. They applied it to the Second Coming of Jesus. He would come again to

158

earth—but no one knew when. He might come suddenly like the bridegroom. His followers must be watchful and ready. Still today we think of this Second Coming of Jesus in the season of the Christian year called ADVENT, just before Christmas.

Groomsmen

The groomsmen at a wedding were the friends of the bridegroom. They waited upon him—just like the "best man" at an English wedding today. But their duties lasted over the whole seven days of the wedding festivities. Because of this they were excused their religious duties for that week. For example, they were not expected to keep either the Monday or the Thursday fast day. It would certainly ruin the wedding week if some of the guests had to go without food and drink.

Now both John the Baptist and the Pharisees taught their disciples to fast strictly, as a token of their love for God. Some Pharisees made a parade of it to win the admiration of men. Jesus did not teach his disciples to fast like that. One day he was asked about it—"Why don't your disciples fast like John's did, or like the followers of the Pharisees do?" Jesus answered with another wedding parable. "The groomsmen at a wedding do not fast. If they did, it would spoil the whole feast. So long as they are with the bridegroom they must eat and drink and share in all the happiness of the wedding festivities."

The coming of God's kingdom was very happy for those who had accepted the invitation to it. The disciples of Jesus were like groomsmen at a wedding with the bridegroom. They could not fast and mourn and be sad. They had entered into the happiness of the kingdom of God.

Going without food. If the fast was more than one day, food could be taken at night.

Matthew 4.2; Acts 9.9;
Luke 18.12; Matthew 9.14

Going without washing

Matthew 6.16-18

Wearing sackcloth of coarse material round the waist day and night. Normally over the tunic but, in great grief, next to the skin.

Matthew 11.21;
Jeremiah 4.8. and 48.37

Placing ashes on the head.

Matthew 11.21;
Isaiah 58.5; Jeremiah 6.26

CUSTOMS

Going without anointing the head with oil.

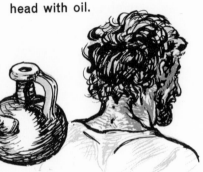

Matthew 6.16-18

Ceasing from work

Luke 10.13

Rending the tunic as a sign of great grief.

Judges 11.35; 2 Samuel 1.11

Reasons for fasting

(1) To please God and to win his pity; (2) To show sorrow for sin and so to turn away punishment; (3) To strengthen the soul; (4) To discipline the body. The Law ordered only one fast—on the Day of Atonement. National fasts were to remember national disasters. Individual fasts were also observed, especially by the Pharisees.

The wedding of a king's son

Another parable told of the wedding of a king's son. It was a great honour to be invited to the magnificent banquet given by the king for the prince. As the custom was, the king sent his servants round to the houses of the guests to tell them when everything was ready. "Come now," was the message. "The oxen and cattle are roasted and all is prepared for the feast." But the guests simply ignored the summons. They went about their business as usual. The king was very angry. He sent out other servants. "The feast is all ready," he told them, "but the guests I invited do not deserve it. Go out into the streets and alleys. Tell everyone you meet to come to the feast." The slaves did as they were ordered. Anyone they met, high or low, rich or poor, was invited. Now there were enough guests for the feast.

That parable is in Matthew's gospel. Doctor Luke tells the same parable in a different way. He says that it was a rich man's supper party to which the guests had been invited. When they were summoned they made excuses—one that he had to go to inspect a farm he had just bought; another that he had to try some oxen he had just purchased; another that he had just got married and could not leave his bride alone by herself. The host was very angry. "Go quickly," he said to his servant. "You will find people in the streets and lanes—beggars, blind men, cripples and the like. Bring them all back." The slave did as he was ordered but there were still some empty places. "Go out again," his master said. "Make them come. Fill up every place at the table. None of those guests I invited will taste of my supper."

God's kingdom was like that. He had called the Jews, his chosen people to enter into it. He had sent his servants, the prophets, to hand out the invitations. Then, when everything was ready, he had sent John the Baptist and his own son Jesus to tell them that the time had come. But the chosen people ignored God's summons or made excuses. Jesus spoke this parable to the religious leaders of the Jews. They were rejecting God's kingdom and others would take their places—sinners, outcasts, tax-collectors, even Gentiles.

Seats at a wedding

Jesus was perfectly well aware of how men behaved when they were guests at a wedding—how they scrambled for the best couches in the most important positions. "When you go to a wedding," Jesus said, "don't grab the highest places. If you do you may be very embarrassed. For a more important guest may come later and then your host will have to say to you 'Move lower down'. How ashamed you would be to have to move to a humbler couch in front of all the other guests! No—do just the opposite! Take the lowest couch of all! Then your host will come up to you and say, 'My dear friend, go higher up the table.' How honoured you will be to be moved to a more important place in front of all the other guests!"

This was very sensible advice. The most important guests always arrived last of all and, if necessary, places of honour would have to be made for them. Those who had to be turned out would have to go to the humblest places, for all the couches in between would have been already taken. But Jesus was not just giving advice about party manners. He was teaching about humility. To be humble is to realise how little we are in the sight of God. Pride separates us from him. "Proud men are put down in the sight of God," Jesus said. "Humble men are raised up."

A wedding garment

A wedding was a very important occasion. Both men and women prepared themselves very carefully. They dressed themselves in their best clothes and wore their finest jewellery. Even the poorest peasants washed and cleaned their working clothes for the occasion. Jesus told a parable of a foolish man who went to a wedding feast in dirty working clothes. He had had his invitation long ago but, it seems, he had not bothered to be prepared for the summons. He went just as he was. This was shocking. It looked as if he did not think it an honour to be invited and cared nothing about his host. Naturally his host was disgusted and angry. "What right have you to be here in that filthy garment?" he said, sternly. The man remained silent—perhaps with shame. "Seize him and throw him out!" the host cried to his servants. So the careless guest was turned out into the darkness.

This was part of a separate parable told by Jesus, but it became added to the parable of the king's wedding feast. That is why it seems unfair that a guest, suddenly brought in from the street, should be thrown out for not being properly dressed. In this separate parable the clean wedding garment stood for repentance. The Jews were like that careless guest. Jesus had brought them the summons to enter the wedding feast of God's kingdom. They should cleanse their hearts to be ready for it. They were treating it lightly and in danger of being cast out from it.

A FINE GARMENT,
SUITABLE FOR A WEDDING

The Jews kept their best garments in a chest in the house, and moths were not unknown (Matthew 6.19-21). They were only worn for very special occasions such as weddings. Then they were taken out and made ready. For a man to wear his ordinary clothes to a wedding was an insult.

If a man was too poor to own party clothes he could easily borrow from a friend or neighbour. Borrowing was very common and quite customary.

There may have been a special custom about wedding clothes. Some rich men, it seems, gave out fine cloth to the wedding guests so that each guest could have a fine new robe made for the occasion. If a guest arrived not wearing a robe made out of this material he would not be recognised. He would be regarded as 'uninvited' and thrown out.

Talents

Many of the parables of Jesus are concerned with money and worries about money. The poor man was worried about not having money to pay his debts and to keep his family. The rich man was worried about having money, for his trouble was keeping it safe. He could not carry it around with him, especially if he were going on a journey, and banks were few. Often he depended upon trust-worthy slaves.

Our first parable about rich men and their slaves is called the parable of the talents. Originally, a talent was a certain weight used to weigh gold and silver. Then it came to mean the value of the gold or silver of that weight. In the time of Jesus a talent weighed about 100 pounds. It is very difficult to turn the value of a talent into English money today. A talent of silver would be about £600. A talent of gold would be about £5,000. These were huge sums of money in those days.

A certain rich man had to travel abroad, Jesus said. He called his trusty household slaves. "I am going to trust you with my money," he said. "Use it well for me while I am away." He knew exactly what his slaves were capable of. To the most able he gave five talents of silver—£3,000. To the next he gave two talents—£1,200. To the third he gave one talent—£600. Then he set off on his journey.

The first slave was proud to be trusted by his master and eager to please him, too. He traded busily— perhaps in corn from North Africa, fine damask cloth from Damascus, and spices from the Far East. By the time his master came back he had doubled his money. The slave with two talents worked hard, too, and he doubled his money. The third slave hid his bag of silver in the ground.

When the rich man came home he called his slaves to give an account. The first slave placed ten money bags on the table. "You entrusted me with £3,000, master," he said. "I have doubled it. Here is your money—£6,000." "Well done!" said his master. "You have been good and faithful in small things. Now I will put you in charge of important matters. I give you your freedom— come, join me at table and share my feast." The second slave brought in four money bags instead of the two he had been given. His master praised him, too, promised him greater responsibility, gave him his freedom, and invited him to join him at table.

Then the third slave came in and dumped his money bag on the table. "I knew what a hard man you are, Sir," he said. "You reap what you have not sowed, and gather what you have not winnowed. I was afraid to risk your money. I kept it safe for you. I hid it in the ground. Here it is." His master was angry. "You lazy rascal!" he cried. "So you knew I was a hard man, did you. Then you should have lodged my money with bankers. At least I would have got interest on my money. I get nothing from you! Take the money from him," he ordered. "Give it to my friend here who had the most money and doubled it. And throw that useless slave out into the night!"

To Jesus some of the pious Jews were like that useless slave. God had entrusted them with knowledge of himself, through his Law and through his Prophets. But these Pharisees kept their religion to themselves. They guarded it and hid it, instead of trading it and spreading it abroad. God received nothing back from them—not even interest. They were cheating God.

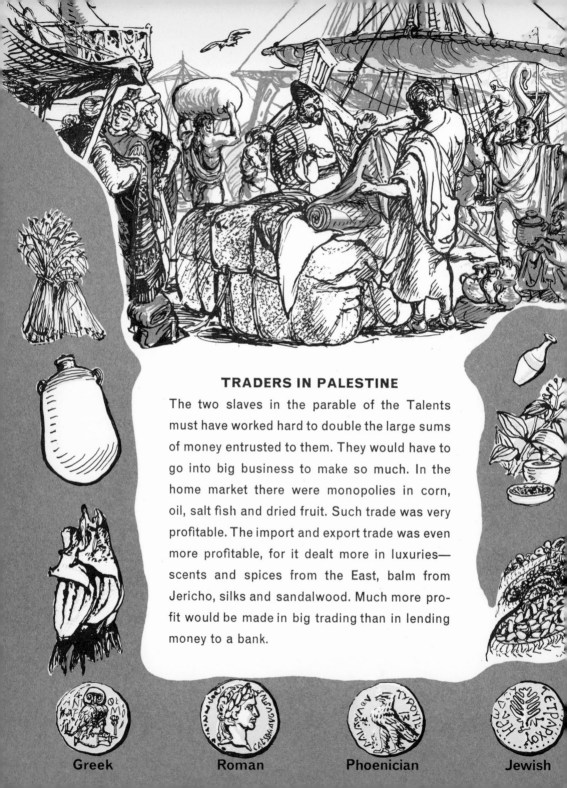

TRADERS IN PALESTINE

The two slaves in the parable of the Talents
must have worked hard to double the large sums
of money entrusted to them. They would have to
go into big business to make so much. In the
home market there were monopolies in corn,
oil, salt fish and dried fruit. Such trade was very
profitable. The import and export trade was even
more profitable, for it dealt more in luxuries—
scents and spices from the East, balm from
Jericho, silks and sandalwood. Much more pro-
fit would be made in big trading than in lending
money to a bank.

Greek   Roman   Phoenician   Jewish

BANKERS

The Greek word used for 'bankers', in the Gospels, also means 'money-changers'. In Palestine there were many different coins in circulation—Greek, Roman, Phoenician and Jewish as well as money minted by the local rulers or 'tetrarchs'. Money-changers were very necessary. They became bankers by lending out their spare money on interest and by investing it. As Jewish businesses spread to other lands, Jewish merchants needed banks and letters of credit. Banks were increasing in the time of Jesus, and wealthy men made good use of them. But poorer folk still preferred to keep their money in the ground.

Bankers were very shrewd and clever men, famous for their sharp wits. Over 70 early Christian writers quote a saying of Jesus which is not found in the Gospels. 'Be good bankers,' Jesus said, 'testing every coin and knowing the good from the bad'. Paul seems to refer to this saying in 1 Thessalonians 5.20.

The unjust steward

A wealthy man would appoint one slave to run his whole household. He had to be trustworthy, as well as clever, for he had to look after all the accounts as well as to supervise the work of all the other slaves. He was called the STEWARD—or, as we should say today, the "bailiff". Roman slaves had no laws to protect them and they were often cruelly treated. Among the Romans a dishonest steward

169

would certainly be tortured and killed, both to punish him and to make him an example to other slaves. But it was very different among the Jews. Jewish slaves had laws to protect them and, in any case, slaves were freed every seventh year. A Jewish slave was one of the family and his master's house was home. Far better to be a slave in a good home than to be a free man starving in the streets. Best of all to be your master's steward.

A steward was a very important man. Everyone recognised him, for the huge keys of his master's house hung proudly at his waist. He had his master's trust and confidence. He acted for his master and represented him. It would be the height of folly for a steward to betray his master's trust and to risk being cast out on to the streets. But Jesus told a parable of a steward who did just that. He had been dishonest and he had cheated his master through his greed and extravagance. "What's this I hear about you?" said his master when he found out. "Give me an account of all you've been up to. Then you can leave my house!"

This may have been a story from real life. The town would be buzzing with the news. The crowd would certainly listen if Jesus brought this latest scandal into his teaching! He made good use of it, too.

The steward had been terrified when his master gave him the sack. "Whatever can I do?" he said to himself. "It's bad enough losing this wonderful job. But I'll never get another once the whole town knows that I've been dishonest. I'm much too old to toil as an ordinary slave. I could not bear to go on the streets and beg, what with everyone mocking me. What on earth can I do?" It did not take the steward long to decide on his course of action. He certainly was not going to take it sitting down. He was a clever chap,

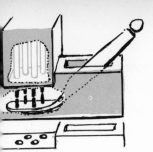

WOODEN KEY

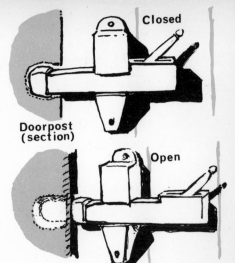

Closed

Doorpost (section)

Open

KEYS

Locks and keys have been known since ancient times. At first they were made of wood. The Egyptians used them in 2,000 B.C., and so did the Jews in Bible times (e.g. Judges 3.25). Still today the Arab peasant uses a wooden lock and key to protect his home.

Locks and keys more like ours were developed by the Greeks and Romans, who made them of metal. Only a rich man would have metal locks. He entrusted the keys to his steward, who carried the large, jingling metal keys at his waist. He wore them proudly, for keys stood for authority and power. Read Matthew 16.19; Luke 11.52; Revelation 1.18; 3.7; 9.1; 20.1.

To close both locks, movable pins fall into holes in the bolt. To open, matching pegs on the keys lift them up into tubes drilled in the lock.

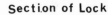

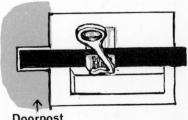

Section of Lock

Doorpost

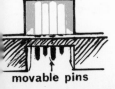

movable pins

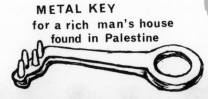

METAL KEY
for a rich man's house
found in Palestine

Keyhole shape

cunning and unscrupulous. He acted boldly to make sure of his future.

The steward sent for all the men who owed debts to his master. They were merchants who bought wholesale the produce of the estate. The steward had the notes which each of them had signed as a receipt. The first one had received 100 measures of oil. This was about 800 gallons and it would be the whole produce of about 150 olive trees. He owed the steward's master a lot of money for so much oil. "Here," said the steward, handing him the note he had signed. "Cross out the 100. Make it 50 measures." Then he turned to the next debtor. "What do you owe my master?" "100 measures of wheat," the merchant replied. "Here's your signed note," said the steward. "Cross out the 100. Make it 80." The merchant was delighted. He owed for nearly 30 tons of wheat, the harvest of 100 acres. 20% off was a very fine discount!

The other merchants were just as delighted, for the cunning steward reduced all their debts to his master. No one would ever know—the merchants certainly would not give the game away! They were not to know that the steward was being dismissed. He was acting for his master as he had always done. They must have thought him a fine chap. They were his friends for life! And that was exactly what the crafty steward intended. Now, when his master turned him out, he could be sure of a good job in any of their houses!

That was the story that was the talk of the town. How indignant everyone was at the rascally trick the steward had played! But Jesus bade his listeners learn a lesson from it. "Why are you so self-righteous about that steward?" he said. "If only you realised it you are in exactly the same position. He faced a great crisis—and

172

so do you. For the kingdom of God has come upon you. What are you going to do about it? That rascal used his wits. He was prudent and far-seeing in his wordly affairs. You should be just as prudent and far-seeing in the affairs of God."

Faithful and unfaithful stewards

A steward was even more important than ever when his master was away from home. Then he was in charge of everything. Nothing showed better what kind of steward he was. "What is a good steward like?" Jesus said in another parable. "He is faithful to his master and he is wise in doing his duties. When his master is away from home he behaves exactly as if his master was there. When his master returns he praises him. 'You are faithful and wise', he will say. 'I appoint you to rule over my whole estate.'"

"But what is a bad steward like?" Jesus went on. "Imagine a slave who is made acting steward when his master is called away from home. He says to himself 'This is my big chance! My master won't be back for ages!' His power goes to his head. He lolls at his master's table, wallowing in his master's best dishes and drinking his master's best wine—drunk most of the day. He enjoys himself by lording it over the other servants and beating them. Then, suddenly, just when he least expected it, his master returns. He catches the puffed-up slave at his wicked ways. He gives him a good flogging and throws him out of the house. That is just what the rascal deserves. For great power means great responsibility. Much is expected from a man to whom much is given."

Jesus was speaking in this parable of the religious leaders of the Jews. The priests and scribes were stewards in the household of God. They lived in wealth and luxury. They cared little for the humbler servants of God entrusted to their care. Were they not unfaithful stewards, behaving thus, in the absence of the master of the household?

Dutiful slaves

The Jews often likened themselves to God's slaves. Jesus used this idea in another parable about a small farmer who had only one slave. The slave would, of course, have to do the housework as well as to toil all day on his master's piece of land. "Suppose," Jesus said, "that they have had a hard day's ploughing. When they walk wearily back to the house at dusk is the farmer likely to say, 'Sit down at once and have your supper'? Surely what he'll say is 'Hurry up and wash yourself and get my supper ready. After you have waited on me you can have your own.' And when the slave has waited on him and fed him, is the farmer likely to thank his slave for doing his duty? You are God's slaves. When you have obeyed all his commandments, you Pharisees seem to think that you have put him in your debt—that he ought to thank you and praise you. What you should say to yourselves is—'We are only God's slaves. We have simply done our duty. All our good works are nothing more than what we ought to have done.' "

174

Watchful slaves

Every slave in the household had his own special duty to perform. One of the parables of Jesus speaks of the door-keeper. He was a very important slave, for no one could get into the house without his consent. It happened, said Jesus, that the master of the house was invited to a wedding feast. The banquet took place at night, as we have seen, and there was no knowing when it would end. The master gave his door-keeper strict instructions before he left for the party. "Keep strict watch," he said. "I have no idea when I'll be back. We might finish during the evening watch or at midnight. But I might not be back till cockcrow—or even the dawn watch. Whatever time I return I shall expect you to admit me at once when I knock. So keep on the alert."

Jesus, it seems, spoke this parable to the scribes. They possessed all knowledge of the scriptures. Jesus had come to fulfil the scriptures and to bring on earth the kingdom of God which they foretold. Thus the scribes were like the door-keeper: they held the keys of God's kingdom. They should keep awake and alert and be ready for the coming of the Messiah.

That was the parable of the door-keeper which Jesus told. But we can see from the Gospels that other details were added to it. This was because the early Christians gave it a new meaning. They believed that Jesus would come again. Thus, they had to keep alert for the Second Coming of Jesus. They used this parable to teach that all Christians should keep strict watch, and added to it details from other parables. Now the master is going on a long journey, not to a banquet. All the servants are told to keep alert, not just one. His return will be one day, not the same night. These details made the parable apply to the Second Coming of Jesus. All Christians must be alert and keep watch for it.

Christians still think of this Second Coming of Jesus in the season of the Christian year called Advent, just before Christmas. At Christmas we remember his first coming into the world. But all through the year we think of another coming of Jesus—into our hearts. That is why Christians must always be watchful and alert and ready. Then, when he knocks at the door of our hearts, we shall be waiting to let him in.

HOW THE JEWS PRAYED

The Jews were free to pray in any attitude. Prayers were usually spoken aloud. Putting hands together for prayer is a Christian custom. It did not arise till about 400 A.D.

In any position of prayer the hands were generally 'spread up to heaven'. (1 Kings 8.54) or 'stretched forth' (Psalm 143.6).

In great distress a man might lie on the ground: Job 1.20; Mark 14. 35.

Kneeling
Luke 22.41;
Daniel 6.10; Acts 7. 60.

Sitting
2 Samuel 7.18.

Standing
In the time of Jesus the general custom was to stand for prayer: Matthew 6.5; Luke 18. 11.

Often the arms were stretched out and the open hands were raised toward heaven: Exodus 9.29; 1 King 8.22.

Bowing
Genesis 24.26; 1 Kings 18.42; Nehemiah 8.6.

References for parables in this chapter

Children in the market-place	Matthew 11.16-19.
The unforgiving servant	Matthew 18.21-35.
The tower-builder	Luke 14.27-30.
A king going to war	Luke 14.31-33.
Dives and Lazarus	Luke 16.19-31.
The unjust judge	Luke 18.1-8.
The Pharisee and the tax-collector	Luke 18.9-14.
Two debtors	Luke 7.36-50.
The ten bridesmaids	Matthew 25.1-13.
Groomsmen at a wedding	Mark 2.18-19.
The wedding of a king's son	Matthew 22.1-5a, 8-10.
	Luke 14.12-24.
Seats at a wedding	Luke 14.7-11.
Wedding garment	Matthew 22.11-14.
Talents	Matthew 25.14-30.
The unjust steward	Luke 16.1-13.
Faithful and unfaithful stewards	Luke 12.42-48.
Dutiful slaves	Luke 17.7-10.
Slaves waiting for their master	Luke 12.35-38.

Cities, towns and villages

Make three lists of cities, towns and villages which you have read about in the life and teaching of Jesus. Use reference books to find out the meaning of each name and write it opposite.

Make your own map of Palestine in the time of Jesus to show the cities, towns and villages which he visited. You can find out the main Roman roads, too, and add them to your map. Atlases and reference books will help you.

Each group in the class can choose one city or town or village visited by Jesus and write an account of it. Reference books will help you. Add pictures or your own drawings to illustrate your story.

Imagine you were a child playing in the market-place of a town in Palestine in the time of Jesus. Write or tell an account of all that happened there, including your own games, of course. You could write a play about the market-place to act, too.

Children in the market-place

Use reference books to find out all you can about the games played by children in Palestine in the time of Jesus.

Make or model the toys they played with. Make a single or double reed pipe, just as they did.

You have read more about weddings in this chapter. Find out what happened at funerals, too, from reference books. Imagine you were at a wedding or funeral in your town or village. Write or tell or act what happened.

The unforgiving servant

This is a fine story to act. Use your own words in acting it. Or draw this parable in a series of pictures as a strip cartoon.

Find a prayer about forgiveness to letter in your notebook or on an imitation scroll. Better still, make up a prayer of your own.

Two foolish rulers

Find out all you can about Pontius Pilate from reference books. Imagine you are a newspaper reporter. Write the story of Pilate for your readers. It will include building the aqueduct and the trial of Jesus.

A selfish rich man
Find out the meaning of the word "hypocrite". The opposite is "sincere" which really means "without wax". See if you can find out the origin of this word, too, and write the meaning of both these words in your notebook.

The Jews believed that, in the life to come, both good and evil will get their reward. Do you believe this too? What do you think heaven and hell must be like? After you have talked about this, write the answers which you would make to these questions in your notebook.

What is wrong with being selfish? How does it spoil us? After you have talked about this make up a prayer for unselfishness. You could make up a story to show what you think, too.

The unjust judge
Act this parable, using your own words.

Look up these references to widows in the Bible—Deuteronomy 14.28-29; Deuteronomy 24.17; Job 24.2-4; Psalm 146.9; Isaiah 1.16-17; Jeremiah 7.6-7; Mark 12.38-40; James 1.27. Imagine you were a reporter on a newspaper in Palestine. Write an account for your readers of the wretched state of widows and of what you think ought to be done for them.

Why do you think Jesus says that we should be persistent in asking God for things in prayer? Is it just to get what we want? What kind of things should we ask for? After you have talked about this answer these questions in your notebook.

Joy: I Samuel 30.16
Worship: Psalm 149.3
Pleasure: Matthew 14.6

Dancing

Anger: Mark 3.5
Reproach: Luke 22.61
Raised in prayer: Mark. 6.41

Eyes

Mockery: Psalm 22.7
Shame: 2 Chron. 32.21
Impudence: Proverbs 7.13

Face

Horror: Luke 23.48
Violence: Genesis 37.22
Generosity: Psalm 104.28
Scorn: Isaiah 58.9

Hand
Beating breast
Blow
Open
Finger, pointing

Reverence: Psalm 95.6
Scorn: Mark 15.29
Blessing: Genesis 48.14
Shame: 2 Samuel 13.19
Consecration: Acts 6.6

Head
Bowed
Shaken

Hand laid on

Love: Luke 15.20
Affection: Acts 20.37
Greeting: Luke 7.45
Betraying: Proverbs 27.6;
Matthew 26.49

Kissing

SHOWED THEIR FEELINGS

Kneeling	*Homage:* Matthew 2.11; Matthew 4.9 *Worship:* Luke 22.41; Ephesians 3.14	
Laughing	*Delight:* Psalm 126.2 *Joy:* Genesis 21.6 *Scorn:* Psalm 22.7; Mark 5.40; Luke 8.53	
Tearing Clothes	*Protest:* Matthew 26.65; Acts 14.14 *Grief:* Judges 11.35; 2 Samuel 1.11	
Shaking dust from feet or clothes	*Unfriendliness:* Matthew 10.14	
Shouting	*Triumph:* 2 Samuel 6.15; Psalm 47.1 *Joy:* Ezra 3.12-13 *Despair:* Matthew 27.46	
Spitting in the face	*Shaming:* Isaiah 50.6; Matthew 26.67; Matthew 27.30	
Weeping	*Joy:* Genesis 46.29 *Sorrow:* John 20.11; Luke 23.28	

The Pharisee and the Tax-collector

Use reference books to find out all you can about the Pharisees. Write an account of them.

Find out all you can about fasting in religion. What is its purpose? Do you think it is a good way of showing love for God? Read what Jesus said in Matthew 6.16-18. Read also Isaiah 58.2-8. What do you think these two passages mean? Find out, too, the meaning of the Christian season of Lent. A hymn which begins, "Now quit your care", written for Lent, will help you. Read it together in choral speaking.

Imagine you were a tax-collector in Palestine. Say why everybody hated you. Read, too, the story of Zacchaeus in Luke 19.1-10. Make up a story of a tax-collector who became a disciple of Jesus. It could be Matthew the apostle.

Two debtors

You have read many details, now, of Jewish customs for eating. Imagine you were invited to a party. Describe how your host welcomed you and what happened at the feast. Give everyone Jewish names to make your story more real.

DIPPING IN A COMMON DISH

This is still a common custom at meal-times in Palestine

Weddings

Imagine you were a bridesmaid or a groomsman at a Jewish wedding. Describe everything that happened.

Draw a Jewish wedding in a series of pictures as a strip cartoon.
Act the parable of the ten bridesmaids. You can also act the parable of the wedding of the king's son.

Talents

It is from this parable of Jesus that we get our word "talent". It means any special gift or ability which we have—for study or sport, for music or art, for speaking or writing, and so on.
Find a prayer about using our talents in the right way. Letter it and learn it. Better still, write a prayer of your own.
Make up a story about two boys or two girls with the same talent. One will use it selfishly and wrongly, and the other will use it wisely and unselfishly. Tell what happened to them.

Stewards

Read 1 Peter 4.10. Christians believe that we are stewards of God. He gives us life and time and talents and possessions. We have to use them as good stewards and one day render an account of our stewardship. How do you think a Christian should use (1) his life, (2) his time, (3) his talents, (4) his possessions? After you have talked about these four, make up a story to illustrate each one. Your story will be about two boys or two girls—or two adults, if you like. One will be a good steward, the other a bad steward.
Make up a prayer asking God that we may be good stewards of all that he has entrusted to us.
Because Christians believe that they are stewards of their money, they use it as they think God would wish. Some of it is given regularly to the church. Many churches have what is called a Free-Will Offering Scheme, and others have a Stewardship Scheme.

Find out what happens in your church and write or tell an account of what you find.

Servants

The Jews often thought of themselves as being God's servants or slaves. But, as you now know, to be a Jewish slave was nothing like being a slave among other peoples. So the Jews did not mean that God is a cruel despot. They simply meant that they each had their work to do for God, and that they should obey him. He was the just master of their "household". Find and read together hymns which speak of us as being God's servants. One begins, "Ye servants of the Lord", and it is about the parable of slaves waiting for their master. Another begins, "Ye servants of God, your Master proclaim."

Other things to do

In this book you have read all the parables of Jesus. Many of them are teaching about the kingdom of God. What do you think Jesus meant by this? After you have talked about this, write what you think the kingdom of God means in your notebook.

You have read many parables about Christian virtues such as humility, love, stewardship, forgiveness, service. Make up a service for each of these that might be used in school assembly. You will need to choose hymns and prayers and readings. Write your own prayers if possible.

See if you can write a modern version of a parable, choosing one you like best. That will make it a story about our lives today. Do this with other parables, too.

Index of Parables

General Index

187

ROMANS	JEWS
EMPEROR AUGUSTUS (31 B.C.–A.D. 14) EMPEROR TIBERIUS (14–37)	HEROD THE GREAT (37–4 B.C.) { ARCHELAUS HEROD ANTIPAS PHILIP PONTIUS PILATE—GOVERNOR (26–36) KING HEROD AGRIPPA I (37–44)
EMPEROR CALIGULA (37–41) EMPEROR CLAUDIUS (41–54)	
EMPEROR NERO (54–68)	HEROD AGRIPPA II (53–70) FELIX—GOVERNOR FESTUS—GOVERNOR
EMPEROR VESPASIAN (69–79) EMPEROR TITUS (79–81) EMPEROR DOMITIAN (81–96) EMPEROR TRAJAN (98–117)	JEWISH REVOLT: JERUSALEM AND TEMPLE DESTROYED (70)
	JEWISH REVOLT: JEWS EXPELLED FROM JERUSALEM 1